D1008637

HAY HOUSE TITLES OF RELATED INTEREST

Books

Empowering Women: *Every Woman's Guide to Successful Living,* by Louise L. Hay

GROW—The Modern Woman's Handbook: *How to Connect with Self, Lovers, and Others,* by Lynne Franks

Inner Peace for Busy Women: *Balancing Work, Family, and Your Inner Life,* by Joan Z. Borysenko, Ph.D.

Natural Mental Health: *How to Take Control of Your Own Emotional Well-Being,* by Carla Wills-Brandon, Ph.D.

The Soul Loves the Truth: *Lessons Learned on My Path to Joy,* by Denise Linn

Transcendent Beauty: *It Begins with a Single Choice . . . to Be!* by Crystal Andrus

Kits

The Best Year of Your Life Kit, by Debbie Ford

The Stop Anxiety Now Kit, by Eve A. Wood, M.D.

The Wise and Witty Stress Solution Kit, by Loretta LaRoche

***

All of the above are available at your local bookstore, or may be ordered by visiting:

Hay House USA: **www.hayhouse.com**®
Hay House Australia: **www.hayhouse.com.au**
Hay House UK: **www.hayhouse.co.uk**
Hay House South Africa: **orders@psdprom.co.za**
Hay House India: **www.hayhouseindia.co.in**

CALM

A Proven Four-Step
Process Designed Specifically
for Women Who Worry

Denise Marek

HAY HOUSE, INC.
Carlsbad, California
London • Sydney • Johannesburg
Vancouver • Hong Kong • New Delhi

Library of Congress Cataloging-in-Publication Data

Marek, Denise.
  Calm : a proven four-step process designed specifically for
women who worry / Denise Marek.
      p. cm.
  ISBN-13: 978-1-4019-1145-4 (hardcover)
  ISBN-10: 1-4019-1145-5 (hardcover)
  1. Worry. 2. Women--Psychology. I. Title.
  BF575.W8M32 2006
  152.4'6--dc22   2006005441

ISBN 13: 978-1-4019-1145-4
ISBN 10: 1-4019-1145-5

09 08 07 06   4 3 2 1
1st printing, October 2006

Printed in the United States of America

Contents

CHAPTER 4:
MASTER YOUR MIND

CHAPTER 5:
PUT IT ALL TOGETHER

Foreword

When Denise Marek's manuscript landed on my desk, I set it aside for a few days, as I had too much on my mind . . . *too much to worry about* . . . to focus on reading it. Never thinking of myself as a worrier, the pages sat beside me, gently staring up, begging for me to read them.

Finally, after nearly a week of wasted energy and sleepless nights, I glanced down haphazardly and caught Denise's simple yet soothing title. I instantly felt it calling my name . . . *"Calm, Crystal. Calm."* Within moments of beginning to read, I was immersed, jotting down Denise's witty acronyms (such as "STOP," a great lifesaver for women who are starving, tired, ovulating, or perturbed), laughing out loud at her personal stories, and thinking of so many of my clients who could use this expert advice.

Every so often, a book comes along that—gently and neatly, as in a conversation with a lifelong friend—seems to unravel the complications of life with ease, logic, and perfectly appointed anecdotes. *CALM* is that book, and Denise Marek is a master at simplifying the overwhelming. Her four-step process will undoubtedly help you learn to relax, release, and let the magic and mystery of the unknown become an exciting possibility. It will literally transform any "worrier into a warrior"; it's as straightforward as that.

— **Crystal Andrus**
The author of *Simply . . . Woman!*
and *Transcendent Beauty*

No matter how much you've worried in the past or are doing so right now, you *can* let go of this emotion. I know you can, because I did. I was once a chronic worrier. I fretted about my weight and appearance, making mistakes, my job, money, and being alone. Was I lovable, likable, or good enough? You name it, and I worried about it.

The strange thing is, I believed that my worry was beneficial. Looking back, I can see how it was "helping" me. Agonizing about my weight and appearance—on top of continually denying my feelings because I cared too much about what others thought of me—helped me develop bulimia. Anxiety over being alone enabled me to stay in unhealthy relationships. Undue concern about being lovable, likable, or good enough helped me not stand up for myself, express my needs, and do what was best for me. Being nervous about money led me to lie awake at night and feel upset about paying bills and kept me showing up every day for a job I didn't enjoy. Sure, worrying helped me all right—it helped me to be scared, unhappy, frustrated, and anxious.

Yet, here I am today—a nonworrier. I'm calm, content, and filled with joy. If I could get here, you can, too! Throughout this book, you'll discover the strategies that *really* helped me. If you apply these same techniques to your own life, you'll stop worrying. It's that simple. I'm not a doctor, and I won't be giving you medical advice. Instead, I'm someone who has experienced chronic worry firsthand, and I fully understand the pain it causes. I'll show you what has allowed me and thousands of seminar participants let go of anxiety, regain inner peace, and develop a renewed passion for life.

This book will teach you how to eliminate worry, break free from self-limiting beliefs, and cultivate inner peace. It's based on my seminar *From Worrier to Warrior for Women,* which has been delivered across North America since 1999 and which contains a four-step process for worry-free living. This strategy is called the CALM process:

C = Challenge Your Assumptions

A = Act to Control the Controllable

L = Let Go of the Uncontrollable

M = Master Your Mind

To parallel the process, this book is divided into five chapters. Chapters 1 through 4 each introduce a step in the CALM process. In Chapter 1, you'll discover that assumptions create worry, and you'll learn the key questions for challenging them. In the next chapter, you'll learn how to use worry as a prompt to take action. Chapter 3 delivers fresh, new strategies for letting go of anxiety, along with some rejuvenated tried-and-true favorites. Chapter 4 outlines techniques to master your mind. In this section of the book, you'll learn how to transform worrier thinking into warrior thinking, thereby building self-belief and self-confidence and eliminating worry.

Chapter 5 puts the entire process together. This is where you'll find Transformation Tracking Sheets. These are your personal templates for worry-free living and can be used to help you deal with all of life's challenges—big and small—with inner calm and peace of mind.

Picking up this book has already started you on your journey toward worry-free living—enjoy the process!

Introduction

Assumptions create worry.

It was 11 o'clock in the morning and we had just arrived in Orlando. Our hotel room wasn't going to be available for another five hours, so I asked my then-12-year-old daughter, Lindsay, if she'd like to spend the afternoon at the Magic Kingdom. Lindsay replied, "I don't want to go today because I have a book."

I could hardly believe what I'd just heard: My daughter would rather *read* than go to a theme park! Proudly, I turned to my husband and asked, "Did you hear what Lindsay just said? She doesn't want to go to the Magic Kingdom today because she has a book to read." But before I had the chance to continue boasting, she interjected, "No, Mom. I didn't say I have a book *to read*—I just said I have *a*

1

book. I don't want to carry this thing around with me all afternoon!"

Lindsay and I both learned valuable lessons from that experience. She found that there are often many solutions to perceived obstacles. (The solution we opted for was to leave the book with the concierge for the afternoon.) I discovered just how easy it is to jump to conclusions and make assumptions.

Many of us do this—after all, it's one of the ways in which we make sense of the world around us. Sometimes our conclusions create a little unexpected humor, as was the case with my daughter and her book. Other times, they create a massive amount of worry. Those assumptions, the ones that cause you distress, often begin as "What-if" questions. What if my kids make bad choices? What if I don't have enough money to pay the bills? What if I try and don't succeed? What if that pain turns out to be a life-threatening illness? What if? What if? What if?

Anytime you answer those scary questions with a negative assumption, an enormous amount of worry can set in. That's why the first step in the CALM process is so crucial: *Challenge your assumptions.*

I discovered the value of doing just that while pumping gas at a part-time job when I was 17 years old. One day a customer pulled up and I ran out to provide the top-notch customer service my boss had trained me to give. While the car was being filled up with gas, I checked the oil and cleaned the windshield. Then I took the man's money and went inside to get his change. When I returned, I flashed a huge smile and said, "Have a great weekend!"

With that, he drove off—taking the entire gas pump with him! I had forgotten to take the nozzle out of his car. The entire apparatus came crashing down, and there was glass everywhere. My boss saw what had happened from his office and came barreling out, screaming, "Denise, go home!"

I left work, but I didn't go home because I was too embarrassed. Instead, I wandered the streets for hours, trying to figure out how I was going to tell my friends and family that I'd been fired from my first job. Of course, I eventually did go home. Later that night my boss called and said, "Denise, you're not fired. I was just really mad, so I sent you home because I didn't want to say something I'd regret."

What can you learn from this story? First, if you worry about making mistakes, remember that I practically destroyed an entire gas station and didn't lose my job. It's helpful to remember that the outcome of our mistakes is rarely as bad as we imagine it to be. Second, I spent hours worrying, feeling knotted up inside and too embarrassed to go home—all based on my assumption that I'd been fired. Let's face it, it was a pretty good assumption! Nevertheless, it was incorrect, and it caused me to be needlessly upset.

Negative assumptions create unnecessary worry. The key to inner peace is to challenge your conclusions before they reach this point. But how do you go about doing that? After all, they're what makes sense to you, so how can you break free from them? This chapter offers six "assumption-busting" questions that will help you challenge your own assumptions and restore your calm.

Whom Can You Talk to for a Second Opinion?

*Gaining a fresh perspective by seeking
another's point of view can work wonders
to calm a worried mind.*

Think back to when you were a child. Do you remember what you dreamed of becoming? When I was little, I longed to be an actor, and when I hit my 30s, I finally decided to do something about it. I sent my photos to a few agents. Three months later, one called to say she wanted to represent me. I was excited, but I wasn't certain I had enough time to pursue this goal. It would be quite a challenge to squeeze trying out into my already-swamped schedule. Nevertheless, I decided to give it a shot.

Guess what happened after my first five auditions? I met some interesting people, I learned the best routes to get around the city, and I didn't get selected for any parts. I also realized that a meager five attempts wasn't nearly a great enough number by which to measure success. Still, those spur-of-the-moment appointments were taking significant bites out of my tight schedule, and I wondered if I was just wasting my time.

I expressed my concern to my husband, and his response was an eye-opener. He said, "That's not a waste of time. A waste of time would be finding an agent to represent you and then giving up after only five auditions." He was absolutely right! It was amazing how one tiny shift in perception gave me an entirely new sense of enthusiasm for pursuing this goal.

To get untangled from our own web of uncertainty, sometimes all we need is to talk to someone else and get a second opinion. Gaining a fresh perspective by seeking another's point of view can work wonders to solve problems, create hope, and calm a worried mind. But be careful—while there are many benefits, asking for help can be a little tricky.

The tricky part is not the *how*—in fact, how to ask for a second opinion is relatively easy. It can be as simple as saying, "This is the situation I'm in, and this is what I think. How do you see it?" This uncomplicated phrase can open the doors of communication and set the problem-solving process in motion.

The tricky part of this process is the *who*. You must be very selective in deciding whose advice you'll seek. If you poke around a beehive in search of honey, you just might get stung! Whether you choose a close friend, a colleague, a relative, or even a casual acquaintance, here's what you need to know before you ask:

— **Seek honest and realistic feedback.** Ultimately, the goal of requesting a second opinion is to engage in a constructive, solution-seeking, perspective-gaining conversation. Don't just look for someone to reinforce the ideas that you already have; choose a person who will provide an honest and realistic assessment of your situation.

— **Beware of your "worry-buddies."** These are those people in your life who fret as much—if not more—than you do. Asking them for second opinions can backfire! Their feedback may create an even bigger synergy of worry and uncertainty, due to their uncanny ability to point out improbable pitfalls and unlikely dangers that you hadn't thought of.

You don't need to eliminate worry-buddies from your life. They can provide a certain amount of support, but if that's what you're looking for, make sure that it's *exactly* what you ask for. Say something like: "I just want your reassurance that everything is going to be okay." Encouragement from a good friend can go a long way; however, there are times when you require more than that. When you really need a true assessment of your situation, consider seeking advice from someone who worries less than you do and who's capable of providing objectivity.

— **Avoid negative thinkers.** Steer clear of asking these folks for their perspective on your circumstances. A "down" force can have such a strong pull that you might find yourself even more confused and frustrated than you did before you asked for a second opinion.

— **Choose an optimist.** The very best person to talk to is someone who balances the "honest and realistic" approach with a healthy dose of optimism. I'm not talking about someone who provides false flattery or misleading reassurance. I mean someone who chooses to search for the most hopeful view in any situation.

A fresh perspective can help you identify and challenge incorrect assumptions. A single idea can show you a way around what appears to be a dead end, and just a glimmer of light cast on a different angle can help you find hope in a seemingly impossible situation. When you need help solving a problem—even the dilemma of a worried mind— talk to someone else and get a second opinion.

Is It Probable?

Reframe the question from possibility to probability, and you'll gain a better perspective.

I magine that you're sitting in the airport, just about to board a plane and go on the vacation of a lifetime. You've planned this trip for months, and you desperately need it. You want to feel excited, but instead you find yourself compiling an extensive "What-if" list:

- *What if my luggage gets lost?*

- *What if something happens to my children while I'm away?*

- *What if the plane crashes?*

After mentally creating your list, you probably ask yourself: *Is it possible that these things will happen?* The answer is yes, of course it's possible—anything can happen. That's why, when we think about the unlimited options of what might go wrong in any given situation, an enormous amount of anxiety can set in. Suddenly, you notice that you're no longer looking forward to your trip; instead, you're looking for the nearest exit!

The good news is that you can regain your inner peace by changing the question. Instead of asking yourself: *Is it possible?* shift the query to *Is it probable?* In other words, you can wonder, *Is it likely that what I'm worried about will happen?* By simply changing the focus in this small way, you'll gain a better perspective. I've found that taking time to rate the probability of something happening has helped me eliminate a large number of my concerns. Try it for yourself:

Step 1: Write down the thing that you're worried might happen.

Step 2: Rate the probability of it *actually* happening on a scale of 1 to 10. (1 = least likely to happen; 10 = most likely to happen.)

- **Did you rate your worry a 5 or less?** That's a pretty good indication that what you're worried about won't happen.

- **Did you rate your worry a 9 or less?** It's estimated that at least 90 percent of the things you're concerned about won't happen. Even if you rated the probability at a 9, there's a good chance that what's making you anxious still isn't going to occur.

- **Did you rate your worry a 10?** If this is the case, you feel that this scenario is extremely likely to happen. But there's hope: The next three steps in the CALM process will help you let go of your anxieties—even the ones with a 10 rating!

When "What-if" thoughts take over your thinking, remember to change the question from "Is it *possible?*" to "Is it *probable?*" This will go a long way toward helping you reconnect with your inner peace.

STOP! Are You Starving, Tired, Ovulating, or Perturbed?

The inception of worry is most likely to occur in the fertile ground of being hungry, tired, hormonal, or upset.

Do you know when you're most likely to make worry-inducing assumptions? When you are:

S = Starving

T = Tired

O = Ovulating

P = Perturbed

The inception of worry at its most "innocent" beginning is most likely to occur in the fertile ground of being *starving* (hungry), *tired, ovulating* (hormonal), or *perturbed* (upset). So when you're feeling anxious, it's important to stop and establish if any of these four "checklist" symptoms are present. If you discover that you're experiencing one or more, the next step is to take control of each culprit by following these suggestions:

— **Are you starving?** You don't need to be literally wasting away to answer yes—although if you've put yourself on a severely strict diet, as many women have, *starving* may be the exact word to describe how you're feeling. Even if you're only moderately hungry, it's quite possible that the assumptions you're making about your current stressors are off base. To help you regain your perspective, acknowledge that your hunger may be influencing your negative conclusions. Then remedy the situation by eating—preferably something healthy, so you don't add to your worry by feeling guilty about what you've just consumed.

— **Are you tired?** "Tired" might be an understatement; for many women, *exhausted* is likely the most fitting word. Feeling a little tired or completely worn-out can trigger negative assumptions. Here are two remedies to help you combat fatigue.

1. The first and most obvious remedy is to **get more sleep.** How much do you need? The most common answer to that frequently asked question is six to eight hours each night. However, in my own experience, I've found that my body knows best. When

you wake feeling refreshed in the morning, that's a good indication you've probably had enough sleep.

I realize that getting more sleep is not always an option. What can you do to combat fatigue if your night is frequently interrupted because you have a new baby, young children, irregular work shifts, or are dealing with anything else that may be preventing you from getting enough rest?

2. **Drink more water.** That's right—this common advice even works in this situation. When you're even slightly dehydrated, you can feel mild to moderate fatigue. The more dehydrated you are, the more tired you'll feel. This fatigue means that your judgment will be off, which leads to more worrying. It can become a vicious cycle. If you've been tired lately, consider increasing your water intake. It will make all the difference in the world.

— **Are you ovulating?** Where are you in your monthly cycle? Are you premenstrual? Are you smack-dab in the middle of your period? Are you menopausal? As women, we know firsthand that our hormones can drastically affect our emotions.

When you find yourself making negative assumptions, step back and check on where you are in your monthly cycle. Acknowledge that it may have an effect on your emotions, and realize that your hormones may be causing you to worry. The remedy here is to simply recognize why you may be thinking and feeling the way you are, and then to put the concern out of your mind for the time being. I know that this is easier said than done, so try some of the strategies in Chapter 3 to help you distance yourself from your concerns.

— **Are you perturbed?** If this is the case, consider writing down how you're feeling in a journal. Keeping your feelings bottled up can affect your physical and emotional well-being. A healthy way to vent those emotions is to record your frustrations. This strategy has helped calm me on numerous occasions.

Once I was on a flight home from a visit with relatives and was fuming mad at one of them. (Hey, as much as we love our family members, they can certainly push our buttons from time to time.) I ripped a blank page from the back of the book I was reading and wrote down every single angry thought that I was having. When I first put pen to paper, I was positive that I could easily fill the page from front to back. However, my rant was only one paragraph long—that was it! Everything I was mad about was summed up in one short blurb. Right then and there, I knew that I wasn't going to allow myself to stay worked up over a measly paragraph, so I let it go.

If you're perturbed, vent your feelings on paper, then rip it up and throw it away. It's a simple strategy, yet it's extremely effective.

So, are you *starving* (hungry), *tired, ovulating* (hormonal), or *perturbed* (upset)? If even *one* of those symptoms is present, acknowledge that it may be the reason why you're making negative assumptions, and then follow the suggestions I've outlined. You'll be surprised by how taking these steps will help you STOP leaping to unpleasant conclusions before they cause your worry to grow.

What Else Could It Be?

Focusing on a positive explanation will help you to let go of worry-boosting, worst-case-scenario thinking.

Your best line of defense for letting go of worry is to deal strictly with *facts*. However, getting them can take time. Between that point in time and your first negative assumption, anxiety can quickly spiral out of control.

A classic example of this phenomenon is the unreturned phone call. Think back to a time when you left a message for a client, co-worker, friend, or family member and that person didn't return your call. What were some of the negative assumptions you came up with about this? Did you assume that the client didn't want to do business with you, your co-worker was angry, or your friend or family member was sick or injured?

When you did finally speak with that person, did you find out that your conclusions were way off base? Perhaps the client had been out of town, your co-worker had been stuck in meetings, and your friend or family member simply didn't get the message. Not knowing what's really going on can create unnecessary worry.

I readily admit that when I was a chronic worrier there were many situations where I didn't have all the facts, and I chose to fill in the missing information with upsetting ideas. If my child was sick, my spouse was late, or my boss gave me a strange look as she walked by my office, I'd assume the worst. I'd torture myself with unconstructive thoughts. Despite the fact that my worst-case scenarios were rarely correct, I allowed my imagination to run rampant and my fear-based thinking to spiral out of control.

Does this sound familiar? Do you let your imagination run wild, causing your negative assumptions to snowball into a massive amount of worry? If this is the case, you're not alone. One common trait of worriers is a fantastic imagination! The good news is that you can use it to your advantage by asking yourself: *What else could be true in this situation?* Obviously, you're going to have to make more assumptions in order to answer this question. But this time, you can make *positive* ones.

For instance, if your loved one is late getting home and you fear the worst, ask yourself: *What else could it be?* Maybe traffic is bad, or the meeting is running long. If your boss says that she needs to see you tomorrow and it has you tied up in knots, what else could it be? Maybe she simply wants a quick update on your workload or needs to know which days you'll be taking off next year.

The key is to think of more positive explanations *before* your negative fantasies have had the chance to build momentum. When you assume the best on a regular basis, worry loses its grip on you. And as an added bonus, you'll often discover in the end that the positive theories are right more often than the other ones.

Changing fearful thoughts to upbeat ones recently helped me when I found a lump in my right breast during a self-exam. My first instinct was to jump straight to the worst-case scenario: breast cancer. To regain my calm, I made an appointment with my doctor to find out the facts. To quell my worry-boosting thoughts in the meantime, I asked myself: *What else could it be?*

It could have been a cyst or other noncancerous mass. In fact, according to the National Breast Cancer Foundation, eight out of ten lumps are benign. That meant there was at least an 80 percent chance the lump was not cancerous. Focusing on these positive possibilities calmed my mind and made waiting for the test results much more bearable—and thankfully, the tests came back clear. However, what if they hadn't? Would it have been foolish to focus on the positive possibilities? Not at all. Worry wouldn't have helped or changed the outcome.

Here's something else to consider: If you're afraid that the worst will happen and it does, you experience pain twice. If you believe in a favorable outcome and things go the other way, you experience the suffering only once! Of course, if you believe in good things and they come to pass, you don't experience any pain at all.

The next time your negative thinking is spiraling out of control, remember to seek out the facts. In the meantime, calm yourself by filling in the missing pieces with positive assumptions. Ask yourself: *What else could it be?* This slight change in your thought process will help you dramatically decrease your worry and increase your peace of mind.

Is It Worry or Intuition?

Follow your intuition; you'll be amazed by how much you "know."

As I walked out of my bathroom, I glanced at a glass candleholder (one of my favorites) sitting on the ledge around the bathtub. I had a strange feeling in the pit of my stomach and thought, *I'd better move that or the cleaning lady will break it.* The possibility really didn't make much sense to me, because she'd never damaged anything. So I dismissed it, left the candle where it was, and headed to my office.

When I returned home at the end of the day to a lemony-fresh smell, I knew that the cleaning lady had come and gone. I dropped my purse on the kitchen counter, where I found a note that said: "Denise, I'm sorry about the candleholder in your bathroom. I accidentally broke it."

Have you ever "known" something before it happened? For instance, have you ever been thinking about a friend, someone you haven't talked to in quite some time, and a short while later, that same person calls you out of the blue? Or have you ever acted purely on a hunch and later found out you were right?

Whether you call it a gut feeling or a sixth sense, what you've experienced is intuition. We all have an inner guidance system, an instinctive knowledge without conscious reasoning. In other words, it's knowing something without consciously understanding why.

Following your intuition will help you make decisions more easily, feel more confident seizing opportunities, and even keep you safe. That's quite a contrast from worry, which makes it nearly impossible to make up your mind and take advantage of the unexpected. It can keep you paralyzed in fear. For this reason, it's crucial for you to understand the difference between the two.

Here's an example to help you tell them apart: Imagine that you've just been offered a promotion. If you accept it, you'll be paid more, but you'll also be under much more pressure. Initially, you're excited about the offer because it's something you've wanted for quite some time. You're told that you have until the following morning to accept or decline.

That night you toss and turn, trying to decide whether or not you'll be able to handle the stress. You imagine how it would feel to accept the job . . . and then how it would feel to have to tell your friends and family that you were demoted because you couldn't handle it. Suddenly, you get a panicky feeling in the pit of your stomach and wonder, *Is this my intuition? Is this gut feeling a sign that I shouldn't take the promotion?*

This isn't intuition; it's worry. If you were to act on this feeling and not take the promotion, you'd be depriving yourself of a potentially life-enhancing opportunity. So what do you do? How can you be sure that you're following your higher self and not fear?

The easy way for you to differentiate between the two has to do with timing. While both intuition and worry cause an "unusual" sensation in the pit of your stomach, it's *when* you feel it that counts. If it comes *after* a series of thoughts—especially if they're fearful—then you're experiencing worry, which begins in your head. Therefore, when the feeling in your belly follows your thinking, it's a bodily response manufactured by anxiety.

If you have that sensation *before* a thought—or sometimes *simultaneously*—then you're experiencing intuition, which begins as a feeling. In this case, the guidance hits you out of the blue and makes you suddenly aware of something that your conscious mind didn't know. This is different from the gut-wrenching jolts that you experience with worry, in that it's not painful, and it breeds calm rather than fear. Experiencing this type of reaction, which isn't tied to a chain of thoughts, is a sign that your inner guidance system is trying to tell you something.

When you get that uneasy feeling in the pit of your stomach, challenge it before acting on it. Ask yourself: *Did this begin as a feeling, or did it follow my worried thoughts?* The answer will help you distinguish between an intuitive sign and a troubled mind. When you stop following worry and start following your higher self, not only will you move more easily through life's twists and turns—you'll also be amazed by how much you "know."

What Are You Afraid of Losing?

Worry is a fear of loss.

After hosting the first five of my one-hour, live television shows, I agonized over the mistakes I'd made. It had been a while since worry had gripped me, and I was surprised by how much these few bloopers were bothering me. Everyone makes mistakes, and I'm a firm believer that I'm entitled to a few of my own now and again without needing to beat myself up over them. So why was I dwelling on this?

It was only when I challenged my assumptions that I realized I wasn't dealing with the underlying issue. Making mistakes wasn't causing my blood pressure to rise; it was what I was afraid of losing as a result that concerned me.

Worry is a fear of loss—fear of losing our dreams, health, possessions, independence, relationships, loved ones, freedom, respect, affection, happiness . . . the list goes on and on. When challenging your assumptions, it's important to make sure that you're dealing with the real issue by identifying what you're scared of losing.

Take a moment to do so right now. Write down what you've been worrying about—weight, children, money, your job, aging, your spouse, relationships, health, or anything else that's been occupying your thoughts. Get it down on paper. Next, write your answer to this question: *What am I afraid of losing?* For instance, if you're anxious about your weight, you might be scared of losing your health, looks, or feelings of control. If you're upset about money, maybe you're terrified of threats to your possessions, independence, or flexibility. Keep writing as long as you can, because you might not get to the root issue right away.

In my case, my initial response was that I was afraid of losing respect from viewers. Digging a little deeper, I realized that my fear of disrespect stemmed from my dread of losing my job as host. Going further still, I came to the conclusion that this anxiety came from my terror of squandering the chance to become a national host. Bingo! I wasn't afraid of making mistakes; I was terrified of losing my dream.

What is it that you're afraid of losing? Keep applying that question to your answers until you feel that you've pinpointed what's truly bothering you. Once you've identified the core issue, you're in a position to challenge your assumptions.

After I figured out my root concern, I began going through the assumption-busting questions from the earlier sections of this chapter. I asked myself: *Who can I talk to for a second opinion?* I talked to my producer and asked for her feedback. Her reassurance went a long way toward calming my mind.

I thought: *STOP! Am I starving, tired, ovulating, or perturbed?* Yes, I was exhausted. There were an unusually high number of deadlines that I'd been pushing to meet, and my fatigue was probably causing me to blow things out of proportion.

Next, I wondered: *What else could it be?* Maybe I was making mistakes because I was learning something new, not because I wasn't a good host. I had to give myself a break. After all, I'd only done five shows so far. Yes, I'd made some errors, but I knew that we all learn far more from our mistakes than we do from our victories. Messing up isn't the same as failure—it's just a stepping-stone to achieving great things. Think of it this way: If you were to take the most and least successful women in the world, which one do you think would have made more mistakes? Most likely, the one taking more risks—the successful woman. My bloopers weren't a sign of losing my dream but a natural result of taking risks, something I had to do to bring me closer to realizing my goal.

Moving on to another technique, I asked myself: *Is it worry or intuition?* I discovered that this was definitely worry. It wasn't an inner knowing that hit me out of the blue. Instead, it was a gut-wrenching feeling that followed my negative thoughts.

However, the assumption-busting question that helped me the most was: *Is it probable?* I specifically asked: *Is it probable that I'd end up losing my dream because of a few blunders?* The answer was "Of course not." That new perspective helped me remember that I was doing a lot of things right. I'd picked and interviewed some terrific guests, and in reality, I made mistakes less than one percent of the time. Besides, people enjoy seeing others mess up occasionally—that's why blooper shows are so popular. Working through this process showed me once again how challenging upsetting assumptions is effective and calming.

The next time worry creeps up on you, make sure that you're dealing with the real issue by asking yourself: *What am I afraid of losing?* Remember to keep applying that same question to your answer until you feel that you've pinpointed the root fear. Then begin to challenge your assumptions. For many of your worries, taking a closer look at your conclusions will be all you need to do in order to regain your inner peace. However, if you've done so and still feel worried, move on to the next step in the CALM process, which is the subject of Chapter 2.

Introduction

Sometimes worry prompts you to take action.

The second step in the CALM process is to act. Taking action to control what you *can* reduces worry in two ways:

1. It can prevent what you're worried about from happening.

2. It can give you a feeling of control over the situation.

In other words, this step puts you in the driver's seat of your life. I had to do just this when my daughter Lindsay was six years old and the two of us were food shopping together. I was pushing a regular grocery cart, and my little girl was beside me, pushing a child-sized cart. As we walked down the cereal aisle, she seemed to go into a trance. Staring straight ahead, she slowly pushed her little cart into the cereal boxes and just stood there with a blank look on her face.

I was in a hurry, so I said, "Lindsay, come on." She didn't budge. I called her again, this time a little louder: "Lindsay, come on!" Still, she just stayed there, staring straight ahead. I walked over to her, stood right in front of her, and firmly said, "Lindsay!" She didn't respond, but a few seconds later, she came out of her trance and I asked her what she was doing. She shrugged her shoulders and said, "I don't know." I chalked it up to daydreaming.

The next morning we were in the car together. I was driving, and Lindsay was chatting away, sitting in the backseat on the passenger's side. She announced, "Mom, I can count backward. Listen: Ten, nine, eight, seven, six . . ." and then there was silence. Looking over my shoulder, I saw that she had the same distant look on her face that she'd had the day before in the cereal aisle. A few seconds passed—though it seemed like an eternity—and then she continued: "Five, four, three, two, one."

Lindsay was proud of her accomplishment, but I was overcome with worry, and I took her straight to the doctor's office. Once there, I walked up to the receptionist and tearfully blurted out, "I need the doctor to see Lindsay right now!" Within five minutes, I was recounting what I'd observed over the last 24 hours. Unable to make a diagnosis, she arranged an appointment with a pediatrician for the next day.

The following morning, the pediatrician told us that she believed my daughter was having *petit mal* seizures associated with epilepsy. She sent Lindsay for a CAT scan and EEG to confirm the diagnosis and rule out any other possibilities. The tests came back positive: Lindsay had epilepsy. We were told that she'd probably outgrow it by the time she was ten years old, but in the meantime, she'd need medication to control the seizures. In other words, she was going to be just fine. I could breathe again.

The point of the story is this: Sometimes worry prompts you to take action. Mine drove me to take my little girl to the doctor to find out what was causing her trances, and the action was effective. Today, Lindsay is 14 years old and has been medication- and seizure-free for five years.

Is your worry prompting *you* to take action? For instance, is concern about your health pushing you to see a doctor, consult a nutritionist, or start an exercise program? Is uneasiness about walking alone across a dark parking lot late at night compelling you to ask someone to accompany you to your car?

Is stress over your lengthy to-do list convincing you to delegate, prioritize, or take a time-management course? Brainstorm alone or with a partner and come up with a list of possible actions that your worries might be suggesting you take. Make sure to capture all your ideas in writing—it will keep you focused and on track.

What if you're upset about something but don't feel that there's anything you can do? Rest assured that no matter how disastrous you envision the situation getting, or how dire it actually is, it's nearly always possible to improve your circumstances.

I once saw a homeless man standing on a busy downtown corner with a cup in his hand—nothing unusual at first glance. Yet there was a remarkable difference between him and others in his situation. As people walked by this man, they couldn't help but smile. In fact, almost everyone I saw pass by reached into their pockets to give him some change. Who could resist? As he stood on that street corner, clinking his coins, he was happily belting out:

> If you're happy and you know it, spare some change . . . *clink* . . . *clink*.
> If you're happy and you know it and you really want to show it, if you're happy and you know it, spare some change . . . *clink* . . . *clink*.

I was happy and I knew it, so I spared some change. Let's face it, being out of work, out of money, and living on the street is one of the worst scenarios that most of us can imagine. Yet, even in such bleak circumstances, this man was able to improve his situation simply by focusing on the possibilities surrounding him.

Keep focused on the possibilities surrounding *you* while creating your action plan. With a little ingenuity and some creative thinking, you'll be amazed by what you come up with. Once again, remember to write down your ideas as they come. A written outline will help you lose your feelings of helplessness and regain a sense of control and inner peace.

With your action plan in place, read the strategies provided in this chapter; they'll help you gain the courage and motivation you'll need to follow through. You'll explore four questions designed to guide you in deciding whether the action you're considering is worth taking. You'll also learn how to let go of the fears that can stop you from doing anything, and embrace the ideas that will put the powers of belief and influence to work for you.

Determine Whether or Not
the Action Is Worth Taking

Only you can decide what's right for you.

Taking action to control what we *can* control sounds easy, but have you ever noticed how worry, doubt, and fear often keep us from taking those steps? So many of us are stopped dead in our tracks by doubt in our own ability, fear of losing approval, and worry about what might happen if we don't succeed—or if we do. Stop talking yourself out of taking action, and talk yourself into it with uplifting messages. The truth is that your thoughts—whether positive or negative—will become your reality.

Imagine, for example, that one step of your plan is to start exercising. In order to make time for the treadmill, you'll get up 30 minutes earlier every day, starting tomorrow. At 6:30 A.M. the morning after making this decision, the alarm goes off. You wake up and tell yourself: *I'll never be able to stick to this program. What's the use? I'm hopeless! I can't do it.* Do you really think that you'll now jump out of bed and start walking? It's not likely.

Suppose, on the other hand, that when the alarm goes off, you wake up and tell yourself: *I'm getting up to exercise now. I can do this. I can stick to my program today.* Do you think that you will have improved your odds of at least getting out of bed? You bet.

Some of the steps in your plan will involve taking a bigger risk than simply getting up earlier. Leaving an unhealthy relationship, having children, changing jobs, getting married, buying a house, starting a business, undergoing surgery, skydiving, or picking up and moving to another city all involve taking a chance and leaping into the unknown. Actions that will impact and improve your life the most are often the most frightening to take.

Should you leave an unhealthy relationship and begin a new life as a single mom? Should you quit the job that's making you miserable and start your own company? Should you undergo cosmetic surgery? These are questions only you can answer. It's up to you to decide what's right for you and whether or not you're willing to take the risk. The good news is that your responses to the following four questions can help you make your decision.

1. What's the best possible outcome of taking this action?

2. What's the worst possible outcome of taking this action?

3. Is the best outcome worth risking the worst?

4. If the worst *did* happen, could I live with the results?

If you answered yes to the last two questions—if you believe that the best outweighs the worst, and that if the worst happens you can live with the results—then the action is worth taking. If this is the case, then affirm with conviction: *I can do this* . . . and you'll be right!

Transform Fears into Action

The times in your life that you'll regret
the most won't be when you looked foolish,
but when you didn't take action at all.

When I was a little girl, my mother relentlessly tried to teach me to never talk to strangers. She'd regularly test me to find out if her advice had finally sunk in, asking, "Denise, if a stranger offered you candy, what would you do?" My response was always the same: "I'd take the candy and then run away really, really fast." She insisted that I should just leave the sweets and make my escape, while I quipped that I could run so fast that not only would I be safe, I'd also have some free candy.

I met the stranger whom my mother had warned me about when I was 14 years old. I was walking home alone when I noticed a car heading toward me. It got my attention because I wasn't on a very busy road. There was a farmer's field on one side and a six-foot-high wooden fence lining the other side, so I saw very few vehicles or other people when I took that route. I watched as the car began to slow down. Then it stopped in the middle of the road, and the driver rolled down his window and asked, "Can you tell me how to get to McDonald's?"

I heard my mom's voice in my head telling me to never talk to strangers, but I was 14—not some little kid. He was asking for directions to a real place, so I thought he must really be lost. I moved closer to the car to give him the directions, but remembering my mom's advice, I stayed far enough away so that he wouldn't be able to pull me in. I gave the directions, and then he thanked me and began to slowly drive away. I walked back to the sidewalk and turned to watch the car to make sure that the driver had understood and was going to go the right way—but he didn't. Instead, he turned the car around, pulled over on my side of the street, and got out of the car.

My gut feeling was to run, but I thought, *You can't run. Maybe there's a reasonable explanation for his pulling over, and if there is, you'll look stupid for running away.* Rather than risk looking foolish, I decided to just walk faster. When I looked over my shoulder, I saw that he was walking toward me. When our eyes met, he said, "I forgot to do something." With those words, I finally bolted. I ran fast, and I didn't stop until I was safe in my house with my heart pounding and the doors locked.

Thankfully, I let go of my fear of looking foolish that day and took the necessary action to keep myself safe. Yet, the startling reality is that I almost allowed that worry to stop me from taking action. If I had, the results could have been quite serious.

Is there an action you haven't taken yet because you worry about looking silly? Maybe it involves trying something new or asking someone for something (a date, some help, or a raise), and you're afraid of looking like a dope if you're rejected. Whatever the case may be, if the threat of seeming ridiculous is stopping you from following through, you have to bust through those qualms— and quickly!

The best way to get over your jitters is to learn to laugh at yourself. Had I developed this ability by the age of 14, I would have run from that stranger as soon as he turned his car around, regardless of whether or not there was a reasonable explanation for his opening the door and stepping out.

Over the years, however, I have learned to view myself with a sense of humor—and it's a good thing, too, considering how frequently I appear foolish. For instance, take the time I was dining alone on my lunch hour and noticed a table of men in the corner. A couple of them were watching me, but I pretended not to notice. When it was time for me to leave, still acting as though I had no idea I was being watched, I paid the bill and very nonchalantly began to put on my coat. I slipped my left arm into the sleeve and swung my right arm behind my back to find the other sleeve, but I missed. I took a second swing, and then a third— but still no luck. Finally, on the fourth attempt, I figured out why I was having such a difficult time: I'd put my left arm in my right sleeve.

There was no way I was getting out of this without looking goofy. I turned to the table of watching eyes, put a smile on my bright red face, and walked proudly out of the restaurant wearing half a coat. Did I look silly? You bet! Everyone does at one time or another. When you appear foolish, isn't it much easier to laugh at yourself than to worry about what others might think of you?

Don't let what other people think stop you from taking action or going after your goals and dreams, because you'll miss out on too many wonderful opportunities and memorable experiences. I almost did. A few years ago, I had a goal of having a conversation with a celebrity. This was important to me because of what had happened when I met Arnold Schwarzenegger. Let me rephrase that: because of what *didn't* happen when I was in the Los Angeles airport and saw him. I didn't actually meet the man, because I let my worry about what he might think stop me from doing so, and it filled me with regret. I vowed that day that I'd never again let opportunity walk on by—especially not when it looks that good!

To free myself from the pain of this regret, the next time I flew to Los Angeles, my plan was to speak to someone famous. My strategy was to dine at the restaurant with the most paparazzi outside, and that's precisely what I did. I remember the evening as clearly as though it happened last night. I was walking through the dining room, trying to be cool and hip, attempting to blend in with these people from Beverly Hills, but with my head bobbing around looking for stars (not cool!). By the time my husband and I were seated at our table, do you know whom I saw? No one!

My heart sank, but I didn't give up. When the waiter came to our table, I asked, "Is there anyone famous here tonight?" He said, "Why yes, Sylvester Stallone is sitting right over there." Oh my gosh! Sylvester Stallone was sitting only *two* tables away! This was my chance to squash my regret and fulfill my goal, so I put my napkin on the table, turned to my husband and said, "I'm going over to meet Rocky!"

But then worry quickly got the better of me. *What if Rocky doesn't want to meet me? What if he embarrasses me in front of all of these people? What if I embarrass myself?* I threw the napkin on my lap and said, "I'm not going." As I felt that familiar regret welling up inside of me, I grabbed the napkin again and said, "Okay, now. No . . . now

. . . no . . . now . . . no." This battle between me and the poor piece of table linen went on for 15 minutes, until I finally told myself: *Denise, you can do it! Don't worry; take the risk.*

Once more, I tossed my napkin on the table. This time, I confidently stood up. I confidently made my way over to Sylvester Stallone and extended my hand. When his hand grasped mine, I turned into Jell-O and sighed, "Woooooooow."

Yes, once again, I looked very foolish. However, I didn't fail because I didn't allow my worry to hold me back from taking the risk. When you're 90 years old, the times in your life that you'll most regret will not be the occasions when you looked silly or made a complete idiot out of yourself, but those instances when you didn't even try. Picture yourself for a moment as you near your 90th birthday. What is it that you want to see in your collection of life's experiences and successes? The question to ask yourself is: *What's stopping me?* Don't let the fear of looking foolish stop you from taking action. Instead, develop the ability to laugh at yourself, and then take the risk!

Aim for Success

*To overcome the fear of making mistakes,
aim for success, not perfection.*

Is the fear of making a mistake preventing you from taking action? If so, the way to move beyond this and gain the courage to follow through on your plan is to aim for success, not perfection. As a recovering perfectionist, I understand that if you have similar tendencies (as many worriers do), you most likely equate success with the absence of any error. After all, if you don't get everything correct, it means you've failed, right? Wrong. A mistake is not a failure; it's simply the outcome of an action. It may not be what you were hoping for, but that's okay.

The key to success isn't to achieve a perfect result each and every time you act. The important thing is learning from what happens—whether good, bad, or indifferent—and correcting your actions until you get what you were looking for.

I discovered the value of learning from my mistakes early in my career. When I first decided to become a professional speaker, I applied to work as a seminar leader for an international company based in Colorado. Four weeks after submitting my résumé and a short demonstration video, I was hired! After profusely thanking the woman who made the decision, I asked her, "Why did you choose me out of the hundreds of applicants?" She replied, "You speak with passion. I can teach people to become better speakers, but I can't teach them how to speak with passion."

I liked that answer. I was so taken with it that I chose to ignore the fact that most other trainers I met weren't keen on delivering the topic I'd been assigned to teach—how to deal with difficult people. Doesn't that sound like a great subject? Teaching others to communicate with the challenging individuals in their lives sounded like fun to me. Why, then, didn't the other speakers want to give this seminar? I discovered the answer rather quickly after I began delivering the program. You see, half of the people who attended the seminar did so because they wanted to learn what I had to teach. The other half *were* the difficult ones and had been sent by their employers to get "straightened out."

On the first day of my new job, I was very excited to present to the 250 people who'd paid to hear me speak in the Quebec auditorium where I'd been booked. I began the seminar at 9:00 A.M., and by 9:15, it was painfully clear who the problematic folks were! They were easy to spot, since they were wearing scathing expressions on their faces that could only mean one thing—*I dare you to teach me something!*

What about the other half? Surely, I could find support among the other 125 attendees, right? Unfortunately, most of the audience spoke English as their second language. Imagine standing in front of a packed auditorium and only getting looks of contempt or confusion!

This was a full-day seminar, and I still had six-and-three-quarters more hours to speak to this group. I thought, *I'm going to die a slow and painful death onstage today.* Then I remembered what my boss had said: "You speak with passion." And I realized: *I'm going to connect with this audience by speaking with passion.* So that's exactly what I set out to do.

When I needed to talk to the audience, I jumped down from the stage to be there with them, on their level. When it was time to change an image on the overhead projector, I leapt back up. During one of my jumps onto the stage, however, my shoe fell off. I bent over sideways to pick it up, which was a big mistake. As I twisted and leaned over, three of the top buttons on the front of my silk skirt popped off! There I was, standing onstage with a shoe in one hand, my skirt gapping open at the front, and thinking, *This is a little more passion than I anticipated.*

Each of us makes mistakes from time to time. When you do, rather than beating yourself up over it, learn from it. Ask yourself, *What did I discover from this experience, and what will I do differently next time?* Life is a process of acquiring knowledge. When you learn from your errors, you grow. For that reason, make it your mission to mess up *even more*.

What kind of crazy suggestion is that? Why on earth would I suggest such a thing? If you're making mistakes, you're taking actions and risks. The more you're taking chances, the more you'll grow and the greater opportunity you'll have to live a joy-filled and worry-free life. Please understand that I'm not advising you to be reckless or flub things up on purpose. I'm simply saying that you shouldn't allow the possibility of a misstep stop you from taking action; and that you aim for success, not perfection.

Apply this positive approach to making mistakes in your life and amazing things will happen. The fear of doing something wrong will begin to lessen, your ability to recover from setbacks will be enhanced, and your inner peace and confidence will grow. When implementing your action plan, aim for success by doing your best to reach a specific goal. If you get the outcome you were hoping for, great! If you don't, pat yourself on the back for doing as well as you could, learn what you can from the experience, and adjust your actions until you get the result you're looking for.

Despite my many, many blunders, this approach keeps me moving forward. It's the reason I'm still speaking today—but never in a button-front skirt!

Believe in Possibilities

The key to achieving your highest aspirations is to combine action with the belief that they are possible.

One evening I received a notice on my front door from a courier company indicating that they'd attempted to deliver a package when I wasn't home and would try again the following day. I wasn't expecting any special mail, so I called to find out who it was from. I didn't recognize the name of the sender, but I sure knew the person to whom it was addressed: my ten-year-old daughter, Brianna. When a child gets an unexpected courier package, it makes me a little suspicious. I thought she must have inadvertently ordered something online, but rather than worrying about it or immediately sitting down with her for a refresher course in Internet safety, I decided to challenge my assumption and wait until the delivery.

When the package arrived, I opened it to find out exactly what we were dealing with. The letter enclosed floored me. My daughter hadn't ordered something online; she'd entered a drawing during a visit to her favorite toy store. She'd won the opportunity to take a 45-second dash through the store with her best friend, filling up a carrying case with everything they could get their hands on! It may not seem like a great deal of time, but when you know exactly what you want and you have permission to just reach out and take it, it's long enough!

Brianna is constantly entering drawings, wholeheartedly believing that she'll win. I, too, believe that there's always a chance to accomplish whatever you're trying to achieve, yet I have to admit that I sometimes discouraged her from entering these contests. At times I tried to deter her because I was in a hurry, saying, "Brianna, don't fill out the form today. We don't have enough time." She'd always reply, "Please, Mom—it'll only take a minute." She's right; it does only take a moment for her to scribble down the essentials.

Sometimes my reason for trying to dissuade her—*as was the case at the very toy store where she won this incredible shopping spree*—was as simple as not having a pen. I'd say, "I don't have anything for you to write with. How about you just leave it this time?" But that never stops her. She'll ask the cashier for a pen, complete the form, and enter the drawing. She perseveres, and it has paid off.

Am I suggesting that you rush out and enter your name in every ballot box in the city? No. However, if you happen to come across the chance to enter a *free* drawing, it's certainly worth a shot!

I also believe that if there's something you want to achieve in your life, you should never give up. Although others may try to dissuade you, and sometimes the odds may seem stacked against you, don't stop taking action. Instead, believe that your dream is possible, and keep doing what's required to bring you closer to your goal.

The key to achieving your highest aspirations (including letting go of worry) is to combine action with the belief that these things can be done. Just thinking about them isn't enough. Let's face it: You can't win if you aren't in the race. On the flip side, acting without faith won't do the trick either; it's the idea that you can achieve your goals that will help you persevere and continue putting one foot in front of the other when faced with obstacles.

Think of it this way: If you believe that a goal isn't possible, you'll probably talk yourself out of working toward it. On the other hand, if you think that you can make it, that will prompt you to at least *consider* doing something about it, which improves your odds of actually *taking* action, which in turn improves your chances for success.

When you combine action with belief, you can accomplish the most incredible things. When I first began my career, I believed that speakers memorized their presentations word for word. For that reason, when I was offered a job doing full-day seminars,

I committed my scripts to memory exactly as they were written. These events were seven hours long, and I have to tell you, it was quite a challenge to memorize all that material. However, I believed that if others could do it, I could, too.

I'd been delivering my memorized presentations for over a year when I met some other seminar leaders at a conference. When they heard that I'd learned four separate full-day programs by heart, they looked at me in disbelief and asked, "How did you do that?" I replied, "Don't all of you?" They shook their heads. They all had their own systems that worked well for them, but not one of them used memorization.

This story illustrates how extremely powerful our beliefs truly are. If I'd known at the beginning of my speaking career that the other trainers didn't memorize their programs, I'm quite sure that I wouldn't have been able to do it. I would have thought that it wasn't possible, and that notion would have transformed into my reality. That old saying is true: "If you believe you can, you can. If you believe you can't, you can't."

Conceiving of different possibilities can help you open doors and shape your future. Imagine, for example, that moving to Italy is something you've often longed to do. One day you find out from a friend that the travel agency in town has a 12-month position open for an English-speaking tour guide to work in Italy. You don't speak Italian and are worried that this might prevent you from getting the job. But rather than letting that concern stop you, you decide that it's at least possible for you to get your foot in the door.

You take the action of making an appointment to pick up an application and talk to someone at the office. When you arrive, you learn that it's not necessary for you to speak Italian, but it would certainly be an asset. You're excited, until the woman in line behind you smiles broadly and says, "That's great! I'm fluent in the language." Her comment makes you feel a little nervous, yet you keep focused on the possibilities and sit down to wait for your interview.

During the meeting, the manager asks, "Can you speak Italian?" Believing in the possibilities, how do you respond? You could say, "No, I can't." However, that answer might just close the door on this incredible opportunity. How else could you respond? Should you lie and say that you can do it? Not at all. Instead, affirm a more empowering truth, such as: "I don't *yet* speak Italian, but I know I can learn quickly."

There's a significant difference between the words *can't* and *yet*. The former inhibits you— remember, if you tell yourself you can't, then you can't. On the other hand, the word *yet* frees you.

It opens your mind and your future to a world of possibilities. In the tour-guide example, will it guarantee that you get the job? No, although it certainly puts you in a better position by demonstrating that you're not focused on what you can't do but instead on the opportunities surrounding you.

The word *yet* goes a long way in opening your mind, as the following story illustrates. I was explaining the power of this word at one of my worry-management seminars, using the Italian-tour-guide example, and my sister Deanna was in the audience. She'd just had a baby a few months earlier and was beating herself up because she wasn't able to fit into her prepregnancy clothes. After hearing me talk about this powerful word, she said, "I'm not going to beat myself up anymore. From now on, when I see those jeans, I'm going to say, 'I don't *yet* fit into those pants.'"

How great is that? Phrased that way, *yet* helped her stop being so hard on herself and could move her to take action toward her goals. After my sister inspired the group with her words, she added, "And by the time I do fit into those jeans, my son will speak Italian." Hey, there's nothing wrong with applying a healthy dose of humor while believing in possibilities!

There's something *you* haven't done yet. What is it? What action do you need to take in order to achieve your goals and let go of worry? Whatever it is, believe in yourself and in the possibility that you can do what you set your mind to. Combine that faith with action and never give up. See for yourself that when you combine your thoughts and deeds, backing it all up with perseverance, there's no limit to what you can accomplish!

Put the Power of Influence to Work for You

That which is beyond your control isn't always beyond your influence.

What do these five things have in common: earthquakes, tornadoes, mud slides, volcanic eruptions, and in-laws? They're all things over which we have no control. Although some of what we worry about—such as natural disasters and other people—might be beyond our grasp, they're not always beyond our influence.

If you're faced with something "uncontrollable" while preparing your action plan, don't give up. Instead, review the following three ways to influence the uncontrollable and come up with some creative action steps of your own.

— Influence the uncontrollable itself. Sometimes you can take actions to shape the unruly factor itself. Take people, for example. You can't control another person's behavior—just ask any mother whose two-year-old is having a temper tantrum on the grocery-store floor. However, it *is* possible—not necessarily easy, but possible—to influence someone else. Having taught full-day seminars about dealing with difficult people, I know that if you take the action and initiative to change your own behavior, you can bring about a change in another's.

This is an option when you're dealing with someone or something that has the ability to change as a direct result of your actions.

— **Influence the outcome.** In many worrisome situations, there are actions you can take to help lead to a favorable outcome. The key is to focus on what you *can* do. For instance, imagine that you're hosting an important outdoor gathering and are worried that the event might be spoiled by rain. Rather than focusing on the impossible (controlling the weather), shift your attention to what you can do. In this scenario, you could create an indoor backup plan, arrange for tents, or schedule an alternate rain date. Taking these actions will influence the success of the event, rain or shine.

In another scenario, suppose you're worried about getting in a car accident while commuting on the highway during the winter. You can't control the other drivers or the road conditions. What can you do? You can make sure that your car is equipped with snow tires, and you can influence how you'll handle the vehicle by taking a defensive-driving course. While some things are unquestionably beyond your control, you can either be *reactive* and let the outcome influence you, or you can be *proactive* and influence the outcome for yourself.

— **Influence the impact.** In every situation there are actions you can take to influence the impact of the uncontrollable on your life—even if it's just choosing how you respond. A young lady named Spencer McBride did just this. In July 2003, Spencer lost her mother, Lisa McBride (who was also my dear friend), to cancer. The death of a loved one, sadly, is beyond our control. Unfortunately, bad things such as this do happen. While we aren't always able to change what happens to us in life, we're able to influence the effect that events have on our lives, because we're able to choose how we react.

Spencer was filled with the desire and determination to make a difference. Turning this into action, she began making and selling beaded bracelets and donating all the proceeds to help fight cancer. She can't control the disease or the fact that she lost her mother. However, through her actions, she can—and is—influencing the impact that this condition has on her life and on the lives of others.

Do you know what's remarkable about this activist? At the time of her mother's death, when she began selling bracelets, she was just 11 years old! It's even more remarkable that this girl is the *senior* member of the entire jewelry-to-fight-cancer team. The group—consisting of Spencer (now 14 years old), her sister, Taylor (12), and her cousins Hannah Malone (9), Kristie McBride (10), and Shannon McBride (13)—has raised more than $40,000 to date. All proceeds have been donated toward cancer research.

How will you respond when life throws you a curveball? The choice is yours. You can't control all of the bumps along your path, but you can decide to take actions that will influence the impact those troubles have on you and others. After all, if a group of children can influence the impact of something beyond their control, I believe that each of us can, too.

If you've been worrying about something beyond your control, ask yourself: *What actions can I take to influence the uncontrollable itself, the outcome, and/or the impact it has on my life?* The answer can help you move from feeling powerless to powerful. It can replace feelings of helplessness with hopefulness and inner turmoil with inner calm. Put the power of influence to work for you.

Take Action for the Right Reasons

Take action because it's right for you, not because you want to please others or avoid criticism.

I moved into a small apartment with my boyfriend when I was 19 years old. Our relationship wasn't ideal, since we had different interests and goals. However, at that time in my life I was terrified of being single, and out of that fear was born the belief that being in a not-so-great relationship was better than being alone. I also thought that living together would somehow magically make things better, so I packed up and moved in with him.

This action seemed to take care of my worry about being single. However, my decision to leave home created a new stressor. I became concerned about displeasing my family, who I thought disapproved of my living in a common-law union. To quell that anxiety, my boyfriend and I were married a year later.

At that point, I'd taken two very wrong turns. I'd moved in with a man who I knew wasn't a match for me in order to avoid my dread of being single, and then I'd married him to avoid my fear of disapproval. I quickly learned that two wrongs definitely don't make a right, and I became very depressed. From the outside, you likely wouldn't have guessed how I was feeling. I was a people pleaser, so I kept on smiling despite what was going on inside my heart and mind. However, there was one sign of depression that I couldn't hide: I slept constantly. I'd drift off everywhere—at friends' homes, in movie theaters, and even in a bowling alley. I couldn't keep my eyes open.

Between the first and second year of marriage, I realized that I needed to end the relationship, yet the thought of getting a divorce tormented me. I'd only been married for a year. What would everyone think? I imagined that they'd believe I was stupid for tying the knot at such a young age in the first place. I had the idea that they'd look down on me for being a divorced woman. I conjured up all sorts of judgmental scenarios, and those thoughts almost stopped me from taking action—*almost.*

I left the relationship just before our second anniversary, and people reacted. Those who had a tendency to think negatively and gossip did just that. The ones who usually thought positively and gave encouragement stood by my side and kept my spirits up. Regardless of whether or not I got divorced, everyone just kept thinking the way they always had, but with one significant difference—I was happy and basing my life choices on what was right for me.

The reason I share this very personal story with you is to illustrate two types of actions. There are things you do for the wrong reasons, such as what you think others want you to do rather than what's best for you. Then there are actions you take for the right reasons, such as doing what you know is right for you. Sometimes those are the most frightening steps to take, but they're also the ones that have the most significant impact on the quality of your life.

I certainly understand how hard it can be to do what's right for you when faced with the possibility of being judged or displeasing others. For that reason, I'm providing you with three strategies to help deal with criticism, so you can take the action that will help you let go of worry and find inner peace:

1. Consider the source. Who's criticizing you? Is it someone you trust, who you know loves you and wants the best for you? Or is it a "small thinker"? There will always be those people in the world who want to knock you down with their negative outlook. Don't waste your energy trying to figure out why they judge you—it's an unsolvable puzzle with missing pieces. Instead, invest your energy searching for people who inspire you, believe in you, and accept you for who you are.

2. Care about what you think of yourself.
You always have the choice between being concerned about what others think of you and caring about what you think of yourself. I strongly recommend that you choose the latter. Don't sacrifice your life trying to please others. As my mom often said: "The people who love you are going to like you no matter what you do. But there will always be some people who *won't* like you no matter *what* you do. You can't please everybody." It's time to stop trying to make everyone else happy and to begin being good to yourself.

3. Look at the bigger picture. This exercise helped me a great deal when I received a less-than-favorable evaluation early in my speaking career. I'd just finished delivering a three-hour seminar and decided to read over the feedback forms before heading home. There were about 100 evaluations, and as I read through them, I was pleased with what I saw—that is, until I got to the middle of the pile and found one that wasn't so flattering.

The participant who filled out this form wasn't a happy camper. In fact, she didn't like much of anything. What do you think I did with her paper? Rip it up? Throw it away? No! I did what many, many people do with criticism. I put it aside so that I could read it again later. I then quickly skimmed through the rest of the good reviews and refocused my attention on the bad one.

Now I was doing *one* thing right in that I didn't disregard it completely. It's important not to ignore the less-than-favorable comments you receive because sometimes, hidden in criticism, you'll discover some very valuable information that will help you grow.

However, it's equally important to understand that one negative judgment, no matter how right or wrong it may be, is never the entire story. Where I'd made a mistake was focusing solely on the criticism. Thankfully, I regained my senses the next morning. I said to myself, *Denise, get a grip. What's the bigger picture here?* The truth was that 99 out of 100 participants indicated they'd learned what they'd hoped to, and many even indicated that they'd enjoyed the seminar more than they'd expected. Looking at the overall situation helped me realize that I'd given one individual far too much importance.

When you're faced with criticism, instead of focusing on it exclusively, as many of us do, step back and take a look at the bigger picture. Ask yourself: *What positive feedback did I receive? In my opinion, what do I think I've done well?* Allow the answers to these questions to help you celebrate the things you did right, and in doing so restore your peace of mind.

The next time the fear of displeasing others or receiving criticism is stopping you from doing what you know is right for you, remember to consider the source, care about what you think of yourself, and look at the bigger picture. This will go a long way in helping you take action for the right reasons, regain your perspective, and restore your inner peace.

Act with Integrity

If you commit a breach of integrity,
take action to fix it if you can.

A friend of mine named Shannon Barks received a hot-air popcorn maker as a wedding present from her aunt. Since this aunt was a particularly close family member, the new bride wondered, *Why would she give me a popcorn maker as a wedding gift? It's not very special.* Not wanting to seem ungrateful or to hurt her aunt's feelings, however, my friend wrote a thank-you note: "Thank you so much for the popcorn maker. We use it all the time." She mailed the letter to her aunt and put the unopened box in a kitchen cupboard.

A year after the wedding, Shannon stumbled across the long-forgotten appliance while cleaning out her kitchen cupboards. She smiled and once again wondered why on earth her aunt had chosen this as her wedding gift. Since she was going through all her cabinets anyway, she took the box out of the cupboard and opened it . . . and her jaw dropped in disbelief as she discovered the most beautiful bone-china teacups that she'd ever seen.

Is there a moral to this story? There are two:

1. Always challenge your assumptions. Had Shannon not assumed that the images on the box accurately reflected its contents, she would have opened it and discovered the real gift. As a result, she wouldn't have found herself in this predicament.

2. Even seemingly harmless breaches of integrity—such as the little white lie about using the popcorn maker—can cause an enormous amount of worry. Imagining what her aunt must have thought upon receiving that thank-you note—expressing gratitude for a popcorn maker that was neither received nor used—certainly made my friend upset!

Compromising your integrity is a surefire way to create unnecessary worry for yourself. Yet, like every other person on this planet, you're human and will make mistakes. Even with the best of intentions, at one time or another you may commit a breach of integrity. I had just such a predicament with a man who worked at the garbage dump.

In my old neighborhood, regular trash pickup didn't include bags of cut grass, so I made weekly trips to the dump each Saturday to dispose of the lawn trimmings. The first time I went, I met a man whose sole responsibility was to direct the garbage. I'd tell him what sort of waste I had, and he'd tell me which area of the dump to leave it in on that particular day.

On that first day, the man asked me what I was bringing in, and I replied, "I have some bags of cut grass, some cardboard boxes, and a bag of miscellaneous household garbage." He paused for a moment and sighed, "Oh, that poor Miss Ell Aneous. She's always being abandoned at the dump. Poor Miss Ell Aneous." I thought it was funny.

The second week was the second time he told me his joke, and I still thought it was kind of cute. By the tenth week, after hearing the same joke ten times, I didn't want to hear about "Miss Ell Aneous" anymore. It was then that I became abrupt with him. I'd stare straight ahead and avoid eye contact. I didn't smile, hoping that my behavior would convey the message that I wasn't in the mood for friendly conversation, and I made sure to not ever say the word *miscellaneous.*

Then one day after completing my weekly drop-off, I thought, *Denise, what are you doing? You're compromising your integrity.* Part of what integrity means to me is treating others with kindness and respect, and I wasn't doing that with this man. I was being rude to him when all he was trying to do was brighten my day. His only crime was that he didn't recognize that he was telling the same joke to the same person week after week. I knew I had to make amends.

That's the key when you have a breach of integrity. Rather than feeling regret or worrying about it, do something to make it right, if you can. I had this revelation on a Saturday morning, and right away I started thinking about what I could possibly do to fix the situation. By that afternoon it hit me: I realized that the dump employee never just asked, "What do you have today?" This very jovial man would ask, "What's on the menu?" So I went home and drafted this menu for him:

Menu
Garbage Grill & Refuse Bar

Appetizer
Bits and Pieces: A medley of late-summer grass cuttings, served with a delicate coffee-grounds mixture and aged over a two-week period in a 105-degree garage.

Main Course
Slops and Sweepings: An outstanding arrangement

of roast remnants in a soured cream sauce, served on a bed of delicately used tissues. This feast is too filthy to forego.

Finishing Touch
Odds and Ends: No need to watch your "waste"-line while reveling in the aroma of this New York–style compost cake. Sniff for yourself!

> *Please join us for some after-dinner*
> *delights in the Litter Loft.*
> *Miss Ell Aneous is sure to help you digest*
> *this debris with her Sweet Sounds of Swill.*

With my menu in hand, I'd never been so excited to go to the dump as I was the next weekend. I pulled up beside him, and when he asked, "What's on the menu?" I passed my menu to him and announced, "Let me show you our specials." We both had a good laugh over it, and let me tell you, he sure recognized me when I drove up after that!

If you've had a breach of integrity, instead of worrying about what's already been done, take action to remedy the situation if you can. If you're unable to fix it, ask yourself: *What did I learn from this? What will I do differently next time?* Answering these questions will help you avoid repeating your errors in the future. In addition, when you learn from your experiences, you can take comfort in knowing that, at the very least, your mistakes haven't been made in vain.

Create your own definition of integrity as one of your next action-plan steps. Allow your personal definition to act as a compass, guiding you in the direction of worry-free living. If you've already compromised your integrity, take action to fix it if you can. A little creative repair work can go a long way to calming a worried mind.

Follow Through

*The pain of regret outweighs the
pain of following through.*

I t's been said that there's no more magnificent
place on Earth to watch the sunrise than on the
summit of Haleakala, a 10,000-foot-high volcano
on the island of Maui, and I was determined to
have that experience during a family trip to
the islands. I was really looking forward to this
remarkable opportunity. Yet on the morning of
our planned excursion, when the alarm went off at
3 A.M., I considered turning it off and going back to
sleep. Before I did, I remembered something that
I'd read about the pain of regret outweighing the
pain of discipline, so I rolled out of my cozy bed
and turned off the alarm.

My sleepy kids, husband, and I piled into
our rented Jeep. After a 15-minute drive to the
volcano, followed by a two-hour drive *up* the slope
in the dark, we arrived at the top parking area. This
was the farthest we could go by car. To reach the
summit, we had to get out of our warm car and
climb a stairway while being pushed around by
strong, cold winds. In addition to the gale, we had
to contend with the high altitude. In fact, a sign

at the bottom of the steps warned visitors to walk slowly because of the thin air, but I didn't take it seriously. I thought, *I'm fit,* and proceeded to bound up the stairs two at a time—which was a big mistake! My thigh muscles were soon screaming for oxygen, and I became light-headed. (But I'm a quick learner, so when I saw a sign in the restroom that read, "Don't drink the toilet water," believe me, I paid attention!)

Once we finally reached the summit—freezing, tired, and wrapped in blankets—we waited for the sun to rise. Right about now, you might be thinking, *Let me get this straight: You flew all the way to Maui, got up several hours before the sun, made a bumpy two-and-a-quarter-hour journey in a rented Jeep to the top of a volcano, where you froze. What kind of vacation was that?!* I think my kids were wondering the same thing—until the sun came up.

In that instant, the darkness was replaced with the most brilliant light. We were so high up that there were clouds below us, and the sun's rays were reflected on the clouds above and below. It was breathtaking. If I'd turned off the alarm and gone back to sleep that morning, I would have missed one of the most magnificent things I've ever seen. Why, then, did I even *consider* passing up the field trip?

There are two reasons why we do things: to gain pleasure and/or to avoid pain. If I'd gone back to sleep, I would have gained the luxury of a couple extra hours of sleep and avoided the discomfort of getting out of a warm bed. It would have been satisfying at that moment, and I might have felt as if I'd escaped pain.

But was that the case? The reality is that I wouldn't have avoided suffering at all. Instead, I'd have created another kind of torment: regret. Unlike the momentary unpleasantness of getting out of a warm bed, however, the pangs of regret would have been much, much heavier to bear.

In the past, I've forfeited the long-term satisfaction that comes from following through on my action plan in exchange for short-term pleasure. I've skipped a few exercise sessions to sleep a little longer, and I've made extra trips to the buffet table instead of sticking to my healthy-eating goals. In doing so, I learned that short-term thrills quickly fade away. The sting of regret, on the other hand, can be long lasting.

If there's a step on your action plan that you've been wanting to follow through on—whether it's sticking to a nutritious diet, getting up early to watch the sunrise, or anything else that requires some effort—remember that short-term pleasure quickly disappears. Yes, the discipline of sticking to your goals and following through on them can be difficult, but so is wishing that you'd done the right thing. The difference, as I've heard it said, is that the pain of discipline weighs ounces, while regret weighs a ton. On the bright side, however, you can use that weight to help motivate yourself.

Here's how it works: When you have a choice between taking action or not, or when you're faced with the choice of either sticking to your goals or abandoning them, ask yourself, *How will I feel tomorrow, next week, next month, or next year if I don't follow through?* Really take the time to imagine what it will be like.

That's what I do when that second piece of chocolate cake is calling me right before bedtime. I imagine how I'll probably feel the next morning if I eat it. That anticipated pain is often enough to help me forego the momentary enjoyment that I'd experience while eating. When you use the prospect of regret as a motivator, the lure of short-term pleasure will lose its grip on you, and the long-term satisfaction that comes from achieving your goals will be within your reach.

But, what if it's too late? What if you're already upset because there was something you wanted to take action on in the past, but instead you let the opportunity pass you by? Maybe you wish that you'd earned your college degree, spent more time with your children, stuck to that exercise program, or tried a new career. Whatever it is, you can relax, knowing that it's not too late. As an old proverb says: "The best time to plant a tree was 20 years ago. The second-best time is now." Maybe you should have done those things on your action plan yesterday or last year or even a decade ago, but the second-best time to do them is today.

The interesting thing about taking action now is that another 20 years is going to pass by whether you do anything or not. So "now" is really the only time you have—which means that this is the perfect time for designing the rest of your life. Today, plant the tree of your future by following through on your action plan. Feed it, nourish it, and watch it grow. It can take you to heights that you may never have thought were possible. Decades from now, you'll say, "The best time to take action was 20 years ago—and I did!"

Take a good, long look at your action plan right now. How will you feel if you begin to follow through on it? How will you feel if you don't? Allow your answers to motivate you. Similar to watching the sunrise from the summit of a volcano, the feeling you get from moving forward and reaching your goals will be one of the most magnificent experiences of your life.

While you're taking action to control the controllable, and while you continue to challenge your assumptions, you're ready to move on to the third step in the CALM process . . . and let go of the uncontrollable.

Introduction

*Learn to let go of worry. Holding on
to it can wreak havoc on your body.*

Worry is a habit, and if you've ever tried to break an unwanted one, you know that it can be quite a challenge. As a kid, I started biting my fingernails when I was anxious or upset. This continued into adulthood, and I began to feel self-conscious about the state of my hands, so I decided to stop. To help me accomplish this feat, I painted my nails with foul-tasting polish, but that didn't work for me. Next, I covered them with artificial nails, but that didn't work for me either. Then I tried some alternative strategies for coping with stress, such as decluttering a room in my house, writing about how I was feeling, or talking to a friend. That seemed to do the trick, showing the truth of the saying "You don't erase a habit, you replace a habit."

That's why this third step in the CALM process is crucial. Rather than trying to delete your tendency to fret over everything, you'll learn proven strategies to replace it, and thus release it. Keeping in mind that worry is a habit, implementing the "let-go" techniques may be rocky at the beginning. Even I must confess that, on occasion, I slip up and bite my nails.

But rather than beat myself up over it—which is another habit I used to have—I use a replacement of positive self-talk. I remind myself that I'm human and recommit myself to quitting once again. How many times have I had to start over? I'm not sure, but I know that it's a lot. How many chances should I let myself have before I throw in the towel? As many as it takes to succeed!

Whether it's worrying or nail-biting that you're trying to stop, when you're trying to break a habit, it's important to realize that a setback isn't a failure. It's just a bump in the road, and every journey has a few of those. The key to successfully reaching your destination is to keep going in spite of it, allowing yourself the right to be human, acknowledging the situation, and trying again. If you backslide while breaking the worry habit, go easy on yourself. Pick yourself up, accept that you're human, and get back on track.

If you're afraid that letting go of worry will be impossible, let me assure you that you *can* kick the habit, no matter who you are, where you've been, or what you're going through. This former chronic worrier did, and you can, too! It will take some effort on your part, but it will be worth it. Implementing the replacement strategies in this chapter will provide you with incredible emotional growth and some amazing physical benefits, too.

Worry is one of the root causes of stress, which has been known to contribute to hypertension, heart attacks, strokes, diabetes, ulcers, back pain, and headaches. In addition, it's widely reported that stress and worry can cause the body to store fat. Tell this to a room full of women and the reaction is almost always the same: "Well, that explains a lot!"

You see, research has shown that stress causes an increase in the body's level of the hormone cortisol. This elevated level causes increased fat storage in the abdominal area. To make matters worse, according to a study by researchers from H. Lee Moffit Cancer Center & Research Institute in Tampa, Florida, excess fat in the belly appears to increase a woman's chance of developing breast cancer. Needless to say, holding on to worry can wreak havoc on your body. On the other hand, releasing it can help you live a longer, healthier, and happier life.

In this chapter, you'll find 52 worry-releasing strategies that have helped me and thousands of women who have attended my worry-management seminars over the years. I'll be explaining 9 of the ideas in detail and listing 43 others in the "Worry-Free 43." Some of them will help you replace your anxieties. Others have been designed to help your body recover from the physical toll that stress takes on it. There are some fresh new ways to help you let go, along with some rejuvenated tried-and-true favorites to assist you in kicking the worry habit once and for all.

There are two ways you can implement these strategies into your life.

1. Read through the replacement strategies provided, and choose the ones that most appeal to you.

2. Review all the ideas, and start implementing one new concept every week over the course of a year. Implementing 52 strategies over 52 weeks will allow you to experience each of the strategies and determine which ones work best for you.

No matter which method you choose, you'll gain the mental and physical relief of releasing tension from your life.

Declutter

*Physical clutter equals mind clutter. Donate,
recycle, or discard those things that
you no longer need, use, or love.*

Take a deep breath and exhale very slowly. As you do so, imagine blowing away all your worries, concerns, and tension. Allow your muscles to relax, and then begin to breathe at your regular pace. Now imagine that you're in a calm, relaxing, and peaceful place. It might be a sandy beach on a warm summer's day, or the woods on a crisp fall morning. Wherever it is, at the end of this paragraph, close your eyes, continue to breathe normally, and really pay attention to how that setting makes you feel. After 10 to 30 seconds in your mental retreat, open your eyes and continue reading.

Look around you. Do you feel the same way in your present surroundings that you did a moment ago in your imaginary getaway? Most people experience a significant difference, because our environment affects our emotions, thoughts, and attitudes. It makes sense, then, that a good way to start releasing mind clutter—such as worry—is to clear your space of physical clutter.

After all, it's nearly impossible to manage the jumble in your mind when you can barely maneuver around the objects in your environment. If cluttered homes and workplaces cause you to have a muddled mind, why do you continue to hold on to so much "stuff"? One answer is worry. Here are two common concerns that may cause you to hold on, and replacement thoughts to help you let go:

1. "What if I need it someday?" This question stops millions of people from getting rid of clutter. It works like this: Imagine you are going to clean out a closet in your home. Bound and determined to get rid of excess stuff, you pull everything out. From this huge pile, you plan on creating two new ones. Pile A will be the keepers; while Pile B will be the discards, recycling, and donations.

You pick up the first item. You haven't used it in years but because it's still in good shape, you say to yourself, *I might need this someday.* So you put it with the keepers in Pile A. You move on to the next item, which seems to be broken, and you think, *I could probably get this fixed, and I might need it someday.* Into Pile A it goes—even though it's damaged. You pick up another object, and you're not quite sure what it is. You think, *One day I just might remember what this is used for, and then I might need it.* Into Pile A it goes. Before you know it, the heap of things to keep is massive, and Pile B is very small—perhaps even nonexistent. You put the items you decided to hang on to back into the closet, which is still as cluttered as when you started.

Sound familiar? Asking a new question can help you break this cycle: *When is the last time I actually used it?* If you haven't used it in 12 months, the chances are pretty good that you won't need it anytime soon. One day you may discover that what you just got rid of would have come in handy. But instead of allowing that experience to stop you from future decluttering, answer this question: *Would I have known where to find it if I hadn't discovered it while decluttering in the first place?*

2. "What if it's worth something?" If you feel strongly that your clutter may have monetary value, why not sell it now and save the money in an interest-bearing account, or donate it to someone who needs it more than you?

A better question to ask yourself, however, is: *What is this clutter costing me?* These things cost you money—to insure, maintain, and own enough space to store them. They consume your time—to clean them, move them so that you can find what you do need to use, and to put them away. They take up mind space, too. What is clutter costing you?

Make a commitment to get rid of three items in your home or office within the next 48 hours. Accomplishing this small goal will assist you in overcoming the most challenging part of decluttering—getting started. As you build momentum and continue to clear your space once and for all, you'll be amazed by how calm and relaxed your mind will become.

Pray

Prayer is the bridge between panic and peace.

Just before beginning a three-day seminar tour on getting rid of clutter, I sat in my hotel room, scared stiff. This was only my second tour as a professional speaker, and the first one hadn't gone as well as I'd hoped. In fact, I thought the initial outing was such a disaster that I *never* wanted to speak in public again. Never is a long time, though, and two weeks later I was back on the road again.

Alone in the hotel, I was still so shaken up by my initial experience that I wasn't sure I had the courage to leave the room. I needed help in a big way, so I prayed. I asked God to be with me and to fill the audience with angels. Then I took a deep breath, made my way down the hall to the elevator, took it to the lobby, and walked toward the seminar room.

The first person I saw was a woman reviewing her workbook just outside the meeting space. I went over to introduce myself, extended my arm to shake her hand, and said, "Hi, I'm Denise Marek, the seminar leader." She looked up at me with a smile, put her hand in mine, and replied, "Hi, I'm Angel." Hearing those words, my panic was replaced with peace, and in that state of calm, I delivered the seminar—and it went better than I could have imagined.

The following day, I traveled to the next city to give the program again. I told one of my assistants about my answered prayer the day before, and a look of astonishment came over her face. She said, "I was just reviewing the list of attendees, and there's another Angel registered tonight!"

Imagine, just the day before I'd been so terrified that I didn't want to leave my hotel room, and now I could hardly wait to get to the next city to find another "Angel." Before my third meeting began, I grabbed the roster to search for that special name, but none were registered. I have to admit, I was disappointed. I put down the list, and just as I looked up, a nun wearing a full habit made her way into my seminar room. I believe that was God's sense of humor—sending me two Angels *and a nun!*

Prayers are answered. The response to yours may be found in what a person says to you or something that happens. It may come in the form of something you observe or even what you read. For instance, while I was prayerfully debating whether or not to write about the experience I just recounted, I happened to drive by a church. The message on its marquee read: "Prayer is the bridge between panic and peace." Then I looked at the van directly in front of me, and its license plate read: "IM CALM." That was a clear enough answer for me!

During those times in your life when you need a little serenity or could use a bridge to move you from panic to peace, consider incorporating prayer into your life. No matter what your faith or spiritual background, this is an effective way to lift your burdens, calm your worries, and connect with inner peace. And remember, when you pray for an answer, you'll get one—you just have to look for it. You may not always receive the response you were hoping for, but you won't be ignored. And sometimes that answer will be exactly what you dreamed of—perhaps some courage, peace from your worries, or angels in the audience.

Act *As If*

Begin to feel calm, relaxed, and confident
by acting as if you already are.

Have you ever attended a wedding reception, business conference, or any type of social event where you were at a table full of strangers? Calling the conversation awkward would be an understatement. I found myself in that very situation during a welcome dinner at a conference I was attending with my husband. There were about 100 people there, and my husband and I were sitting at a table with four couples whom we didn't know.

After some introductory small talk, I said to the group, "If you're up for playing a game, I know a way to guarantee we'll have more fun at our table than anyone else in the room. Here's how it works: Throughout dinner, we all have to act *as if* we're having a great time. For instance, every time someone tells a joke, even if it's a groaner, we all have to laugh *as if* it's the funniest thing we've ever heard."

My dinner companions probably thought I was off my rocker at that point, but thankfully, someone started the game by telling a joke. It was pretty lame, but we all whooped and cheered anyway. That gave another person the confidence to relate a funny story, and again, we laughed as hard as we would have if it had been the funniest thing we'd ever heard.

I know this sounds strange, but gradually everyone at the table started to relax. We lost our fear of looking foolish and stopped worrying about what other people might think of us, because we knew that even if we said something silly or if our anecdote was boring, it would still be well received. As a bonus, after the first few times of forcing ourselves to laugh, things actually got pretty funny. The more we giggled, and the more we saw others doing the same, the funnier it became.

Remember the adage "Fake it till you make it"? We started out by acting *as if* we were having fun and before we knew it, we actually were. Even more interesting, on the following day, many of the other conference attendees came over to our group, saying things like, "You were so lucky to be at the fun table. Last night we wished we were sitting with you."

Here's something to think about: If you can have fun by simply acting *as if* you're having a great time, isn't it possible that there are other life applications for this technique? For instance, what if you acted as if you were relaxed in order to combat nervousness? What if, to deal with worry, you behaved as if you were calm? What if you imitated a confident person in order to eradicate low self-esteem? Eventually, you'd move from acting as if you were relaxed, calm, and confident to actually feeling that way.

Is it a good idea to behave as if you're in perfect health when you're having chest pains? Is it wise to act as though your relationship is great when in fact it's abusive, or to pretend that your car is in perfect working order when it's actually falling apart and you're planning a cross-country road trip? Of course not. In these cases, you need to take action to address these issues.

Acting *as if* is a good strategy to employ during those situations where you aren't in any danger and want to shift how you're feeling. When you're stressed, bored, anxious, insecure, or experiencing any other uncomfortable sensation, you can improve things and transform your mood and experience. Simply act *as if* you already feel the way you want to.

Why not try it yourself and *act* your way out of worry and into feeling calm. Don't be concerned if the transformation isn't immediate. Even at that conference dinner table, it took four or five rounds of forced laughter before it was no longer an act and real merriment took over. Just stick with it, and you can be relaxed and confident by acting *as if* you already are.

∽⧖∾

Ink It

Release pent-up worry with the stroke of a pen.

One of the simplest ways to banish stress in mere minutes is by putting pen to paper. Writing about your worries is an effective way to let them go and calm your mind. It's a mental detoxification process that allows you to dump your concerns onto the page, creating the space needed for new insights that will help you deal with those issues. You can't gain this perspective by just *thinking* about your troubles; you must get them out and *look* at them. Only then can you decide what to keep and what to discard.

If you're like many women and have written the words "Dear Diary" at the top of a blank page, you know precisely how powerful this process can be. It's important, however, to understand the difference between journaling—specifically for worry management—and keeping a diary. Unlike those notebooks, where you record the events happening in your life, the key in journaling to reduce anxiety is writing about how the events in your life make you *feel*.

One of the best ways to get the pen rolling is to begin with the phrase "Today I felt . . ." Don't be too surprised if this task is uncomfortable at first. Many people spend an inordinate amount of time trying to suppress and avoid anxious feelings, so give yourself some time to allow your emotions to surface. They may be buried very deep! Get comfortable and say to yourself, *I'm going to sit here for the next 10 or 15 minutes, and I'm going to write. I'm going to do more than list events. I'm going to take away layer after layer of thoughts, distractions, concerns, and perceptions until I uncover my true feelings.*

Initially, excavating what you're really experiencing may seem to create more mental clutter than it clears. However, journaling is similar to cleaning out a really messy closet: You first have to pull everything out of the space. If you were to stop there, it would look as if you'd just made an even bigger mess. Yet as you discard those things that no longer serve you and deal with those that do, it quickly becomes apparent that you're creating a fresh new space. The initial mess was a worthwhile and necessary part of the process.

Along with helping you let go of worry, journaling also gives you the opportunity to vent your true feelings, divulge your innermost thoughts, and express your concerns without ever being judged or interrupted. It's interesting, however, that many people will still be careful about what they write because they're worried that someone else is going to find the journal. Obviously, repressing your emotions by censoring your writing defeats the purpose, but the good news is that you don't need to keep what you've written in order to receive the blessings of this process. In fact, you can scrawl your true feelings down on paper, tear it up and throw it out, and still reap the rewards of reduced worry. Your brain keeps the benefits of the "closet cleaning" without having to hold on to the garbage bags.

Please remember, if writing about your feelings becomes too painful or emotionally overwhelming at any point, you may wish to seek professional assistance. Your first instinct might be to quit and ignore your emotions, but sweeping them under the rug won't help. They're an indication that you've hit on something that needs your attention. Getting professional help to deal with those issues can help you let go of worry and truly move forward in your life.

After 10 to 15 minutes of writing about your feelings and concerns, end your journal on a positive note by listing three to five things for which you're grateful. Shifting your attention to what you appreciate will help you refocus your thinking, regain your perspective, and remember that there's more to your life than what's currently preoccupying you.

The next time anxiety hits, grab a pen and write it out. As you look inside yourself and uncover your true feelings, you'll be amazed by how much more calm and content you become. "Ink it" to help yourself reconnect with the peace and joy that worry crowds out.

Find and Utilize
Your Unique Abilities

*Using your unique ability will add a dimension
of pleasure and peace to your life that you may
never have imagined possible.*

My friend Lisa had been undergoing cancer treatments for about four years when she told me over the phone about a wonderful soup that a friend of hers had made. During that conversation, Lisa told me that her friend had been bringing her homemade soup every week since her cancer treatments had begun. I was really glad someone had been making her tasty meals, but at the same time I felt bad that I hadn't thought of it myself. I said, "Lisa, I'm so sorry I didn't make you soup." She replied, "But Denise, you make me *laugh*."

She reminded me of two important truths that day:

1. We all have our own unique abilities.

2. It's important to let go of trying to be good at everything.

Let's face it—no one excels at *everything*. However, each of us is good at *something*. When you let go of trying to do it all perfectly, your time and energy are freed up to develop, appreciate, and use that special talent that's uniquely yours.

It's imperative to know what you're good at and to utilize it. This is one of the ways to build pleasure into your life—there's no denying the joy that comes from doing what you love and doing it well. There's an added benefit, too: Using your gift can help you stop worrying about the future and regretting the past, because it totally immerses you in the present moment. When you learn to live fully in the present, the uncertainty of tomorrow and the dissatisfaction of yesterday melt away.

If you're not sure what your *something* is yet, a great way to begin the search is to remember your childhood. Think back to when you were a kid. What did you enjoy doing the most? If you can't recall, look back through old photos; the clues they can provide are amazing.

I experienced this firsthand one Christmas when my daughter Lindsay gave me a homemade scrapbook. One of the pictures in it showed me at 12 years old, standing in front of a bulletin board. The display included awards I'd won in elementary school, including three public-speaking honors. This surprised me, because I didn't remember winning them—but I now make my living as a professional speaker! While I don't recall those events, I certainly remember talking so much that adults would pay me to be quiet! Your childhood can probably also provide many clues as to what your natural abilities are.

Abraham Maslow, creator of the famous hierarchy of needs, wrote: "A musician must make music, an artist must paint, a poet must write, if he is to be ultimately at peace with himself. What a man can be, he must be." And the same is true for women! Take a moment now to ask yourself what *you* must be: What unique gift is in your possession? Are you talented in business? Do you have "the gift of the gab"? Do you excel at sports? Can you cut a rug like nobody else?

If you don't think that you have a unique ability, let me reassure you that you do. Remember, each one of us is good at *something*. Once you've determined your gift, find ways to express it. Whether you can cook the most marvelous soups, make people laugh, or offer some other equally valuable contribution, use your talent and share it with others. It will add a dimension of pleasure and peace to your life that you may never have thought possible!

Extend Kindness to Another

*You have the power to boost your mood anytime you
choose simply by extending kindness to another.*

I was at the information center in Disney World
and overheard a panicking man with a thick
Australian accent telling an employee that he'd lost
his wallet and passport. As he was verbally retracing
his steps, an American man arrived at the counter
beside him to turn in a wallet and Australian
passport that he'd found near one of the rides.
The relief and gratitude that the first gentleman
expressed to the second was so amazing that when
I went on my way, I was on a high. Even though
I wasn't the one who returned the missing items,
nor the one reunited with my lost property, I felt
incredible—why?

According to Dr. Wayne W. Dyer in his book
The Power of Intention, acts of kindness can cause
your brain to increase the production of serotonin.
This neurotransmitter (a type of body chemical)
can help reduce depression and make you feel
peaceful and euphoric. Dr. Dyer writes that not
only is the production of this substance increased
in both the recipient and the giver of kindness,
but also in people observing the act. I was feeling

euphoric because my serotonin levels had gone up as a result of what I'd observed. How does this chemical reaction help you let go of worry? Just try feeling elated and worried at the same time. It's virtually impossible!

After reading that section of Dr. Dyer's book, I went on an "act-of-kindness" spree to see if I could experience that wonderful feeling again. One target for my actions was my daughter Brianna's fifth-grade teacher. Before picking up Brianna from school, I stopped at a flower shop and bought a bouquet of flowers. I brought them into the classroom and presented them to the teacher. Her eyes opened wide, and she asked, "Do you know what day it is?" I said that I didn't. She replied, "Today is my birthday." With those words, I think my serotonin levels quadrupled. I felt like I was on top of the world.

Could you use a boost in your mood? If so, start thinking of ways you can extend kindness to others. Get creative and have some fun with it. For instance, you could put a quarter in the change slot of a phone booth or gumball machine. Just imagine the pleasure that will bring to the person who finds your surprise. If you're in line at the grocery store with a full cart, and whoever is behind you only has a few items, you could let that person ahead of you. Or maybe you could do something for the planet by recycling more items or by planting a tree. Any act of kindness on your part, no matter how small, will be returned in the form of happiness. Look for ways to be good to others in your life, and those wonderful feelings will go a long way in helping you let go of worry. Try it yourself—you'll be amazed by the results!

Ask for Help

Learn to ask for help when you need it,
and accept it when it's offered.

My husband, Terry, was driving through a busy intersection when he noticed a duck in the middle of the road. This poor bird had obviously been hit by a car and was now on its back, frantically kicking its feet in the air, trying to right itself as it helplessly watched vehicles zoom by. Terry knew that if he didn't get this creature out of there, it was going to be squashed.

Terry pulled to the side of the road, ran over to pick up the duck, and brought it back to his van. He could tell that its wing had been injured, so he drove to a nearby animal hospital, but it was closed. So he went on to another facility across town, which was open, but when he walked through the door, he was told: "We don't do ducks."

Determined to help save the bird, Terry took it back to his office and called the local wildlife foundation. They were happy to help and asked if he'd come see them the following day. Relieved, he said yes. In the meantime, the duck needed a place to stay, so he brought it to our house for the night, safely contained in a large blanketed box. Early the next morning, he made the one-hour drive to the wildlife foundation, and having helped as much as he could, said his good-byes and left it in their capable hands.

Before Terry left to make his kindhearted delivery that morning, I had one last peek inside the box. As I watched the duck resting, I thought about the ordeal it had been through over the previous 12 hours. It struck me that I knew how it must have felt on its back in the middle of the road. I, too, have felt as though I were upside down with my feet kicking in the air. However, it wasn't a car that knocked me flying, it was my to-do list—and it wasn't passing vehicles but the days that were zooming by!

Do you sometimes feel that way? Does it sometimes seem as if there's too much to do and too little time? Do you helplessly watch the weeks fly by, feeling that at any moment you're going to be squashed? If so, you're not alone. Women typically have multiple roles—caregiver, mother, business owner, employee, community activist, spouse, partner, friend—the list goes on and on. It can be extremely challenging and often overwhelming to balance work and family obligations. Being overloaded can exhaust you physically and mentally, and that's precisely when worry is likely to take hold. The good news is that you can get out of the busy intersection safely. Sometimes you just need a little assistance.

Each of us could use a little help—or a lot—from time to time. But for some strange reason, many of us don't ask for it, or worse yet, won't accept it, even when it's offered on a silver platter. I used to pretend that I didn't need assistance from others, and many women do the same thing. For me, it was partially about giving up control. I once lived by the belief that "if you want something done right, you have to do it yourself." Over the years, however, I've come to discover that at certain times, if you want to get a thing done *at all,* you have to let someone else take care of it.

How do you give up the need for control and accept the help you require to knock some items off your task list before the list knocks you over? Strive for *progress* rather than *perfection.* I'll be the first to admit that when you accept someone else's assistance in accomplishing a task, things may not be done exactly the way you would have liked. Sometimes, however, they'll be better than you could have done on your own. Either way, they'll be completed, and you can move on.

I was also hesitant to accept offers from others because I was afraid to admit that I couldn't do everything. I thought it somehow meant I was incompetent. Here's a news flash: Asking for help doesn't mean you're incompetent, just human. Don't let your misperceptions fool you. No one's able to do everything alone all the time. In fact, that line of thinking will set you up for disaster. Instead, set yourself up for success by considering a truth I've adopted for myself: *I can do <u>anything</u>, just not <u>everything</u>.* You really can accomplish whatever you want to, but sometimes, like that duck, you just need a little help along the way.

Remember: If you feel as if you've been knocked upside down by your to-do list, strive for progress not perfection. Ask for assistance if you need it, and accept when it's offered. That helping hand may be all you need to get back on your feet, out of the busy intersection, and into the driver's seat of your life.

Make Peace with Your Past

*To stop worrying about your past, you
first need to make peace with it.*

Imagine that you're packing your bags to return home from vacation and you're having a difficult time trying to squeeze everything into your suitcase. Before you left for your trip, you planned carefully and managed to fit everything neatly and easily. Now, however, it's a completely different story. While you were away, you picked up some treats and treasures to help you remember the trip. You purchased gifts for loved ones and bought a few new articles of clothing. As a result, you're now finding it nearly impossible to cram everything into your bag. This has happened to me, and in fact, I've even gone so far as to purchase an extra suitcase while I was away so that I could finish packing!

Over the years, I've recognized that our vacation baggage and emotional baggage are similar. Everything fits when we begin our life's journey. We have a clean slate, an open mind, and are ready to go out and experience the world, but as time passes, we begin to accumulate things. We gather experiences, lessons, perceptions, ideas, beliefs, and other weighty items. At the end of our trip, just as with the vacation, we're left with more than we started.

While there's a similarity between your emotional and vacation baggage, however, there's also a significant difference. After a long trip, you eventually unpack your bags. You give the gifts to your loved ones; you wash your clothes and put them back in your closet. You eat the treats, display the mementos, and develop the film. Away your suitcase goes, empty and ready for your next adventure.

Our emotions, on the other hand, never seem to get unpacked. We keep our regrets, mistakes, and perceived flaws stuffed inside. We keep our pain locked up tight until we're bursting at the seams. Eventually, this "suitcase" becomes so heavy and full that it crowds out happiness. To reconnect with your joy and stop worrying about the past, you need to make peace with it. You need to unpack your emotional baggage.

I learned how to do this from my friend Sally Walker. She worked at a homeless shelter, and one day, she cooked better soup than she ever had before. She thought, *This is fantastic! It smells and tastes great—it's the best soup I've ever made.* While serving it with some warm bread to the people who'd come to the shelter that day, she marveled at just how wonderful her creation was. Not too long into her shift, a little old lady at the back of the kitchen called over to Sally, asking her to come back and speak with her. It was Mother Teresa!

Sally thought, *Oh, I know what this is about. Mother Teresa has tasted my soup! She wants to tell me how good it is.* She happily approached the holy woman, who said, "Look at the way you're serving these people with disgust. Can't you see that everyone is broken? Some people are broken on the outside where everyone can see it, and some people are broken on the inside, but *everybody* is broken. Imagine taking all of these broken pieces and putting them together to form a beautiful, beautiful mosaic. You need to go home until you can see that beautiful mosaic."

Sally was shocked. She could hardly believe that she'd just been sent home from the soup kitchen by Mother Teresa. Later that night, she thought about what she'd been told. *Had* she been serving the people with disgust? She realized that, unintentionally, she had. Sometimes she'd think, *Oh, please don't touch me—you're so dirty,* or *Please move up the line quickly; you smell bad.* All she'd seen was their brokenness, but that evening she began to see the beautiful mosaic.

When I heard Sally's powerful story, I realized that I wasn't alone, because Mother Teresa's words described every human being. We all have emotional baggage. Some wear it on the outside where it's easy to see, and others keep it hidden deep inside. Whether it's visible or not, we're all broken.

Do you realize what this means? You don't need to hide your faults away in shame or beat yourself up for the mistakes you've made. You're just like every single person on this planet—a part of the beautiful mosaic! Herein lies the key to making peace with your past: Forgive yourself. Don't judge yourself harshly for past missteps. You're not alone; we're all part of the beautiful mosaic. It's time to unpack your emotional baggage and make room for a new great adventure.

Have Faith in Happy Endings

*Calm your mind today by imagining
the best for tomorrow.*

I remember being in the hospital when I was a girl, in excruciating pain with a horribly infected leg. Four days earlier, I'd somehow managed to plunge a steak knife deep into the side of my right knee. I was 12 years old and hadn't been concentrating on what I was doing, until I realized I had a knife sticking out of me. I yanked it loose and screamed for my older sister to call an ambulance. She wrapped my leg with a tea towel as a tourniquet and called my mother at work to come take me to the hospital. There I had my wound bandaged up and was sent home.

The next day, my knee really started to hurt. I was limping around the house and complaining about the pain to my family, who all thought I was laying it on thick just to get attention. My wound hadn't even required stitches, so it was a fairly reasonable assumption. However, it was incorrect. I wasn't exaggerating, and by the end of the third day, my knee had more than doubled in size. I was in so much pain that I couldn't get out of bed, and by then it was very obvious that I wasn't just playing for sympathy.

As I was unable to move without screaming in agony, my mom called an ambulance to take me to the hospital. The paramedics arrived, saw how much pain I was in, and suggested that my mother just pack the joint in ice rather than try to move me. They assumed there wasn't anything seriously wrong with me, and all I required was some ice to bring down the swelling—another incorrect assumption. The next morning, after having been iced for the night, my knee was even worse, swollen to a size bigger than my head.

"This is ridiculous," my stepfather said. "I'll take you to the hospital myself." While I cried, he and my mom carried me down the stairs of our house and drove me back to the hospital. The admitting nurse took one look at me, rushed me into an examination room, and within a matter of minutes, a swarm of doctors were hovering over my leg. I was relieved to finally be getting the help I needed. I was sure that I'd be fixed up in no time. Little did I know that the doctor was out in the hallway, telling my mom that my leg would likely have to be amputated. That had never even crossed my mind. At the age of 12, I believed that people went to the hospital to get better, not to get things cut off!

Thankfully, my mom wasn't keen on the idea and asked them to first do everything possible to save my leg. They agreed to treat it with intravenously administered antibiotics, but warned that they'd only be able to use that course of action for a short time before running the risk of the infection spreading. An operation was also scheduled for the following day to drain some of the fluid, and I was admitted to a hospital room. Even though the pain was unbearable, I took comfort in knowing that I'd be better soon.

After a night of medication, the swelling started to subside, and the operation was postponed 24 hours. On the third day I was there, I was still unable to move my leg without a huge amount of pain, but my knee *was* getting better. The doctors were astonished. The operation was put off another day, then another and another. A week later, without surgery, I'd healed and was released from the hospital. With the help of crutches—and with *both* of my legs still attached—I hobbled home. After a month, I was running around as though the entire ordeal had never occurred. Only then did my mom explain just how close I'd come to having an amputation.

This experience once again illustrates the value of challenging your assumptions. Incorrect beliefs almost cost me my leg. However, there's another equally important message, and that is to have faith in happy endings. They happen all the time:

- A woman with cancer hears from her
  doctor that the disease is in remission.

- A woman who's had difficulty conceiving
  finds out that she's pregnant or adopts her
  first child.

- A woman who's been told that she'd
  never walk again leaves her wheelchair
  and takes her first few steps.

- My own mother, who'd been told that
  her child's leg might have to be amputated, believed in the possibility of happy
  endings when she asked the doctors to
  first do whatever they could to avoid that
  outcome. One month later, she watched
  that same child run around on two
  healthy legs.

When you find yourself smack-dab in the
middle of a worrisome situation, calm your mind
by acknowledging that it's just as possible that a
happy ending can occur for you, too.

It's important to understand that I'm not asking
you to believe in a fairy-tale "happily ever after"
ending, where the prince and princess spend the
rest of their lives in uninterrupted harmony. We all

know that along with the triumphs, victories, joy, and bliss of the real world, we'll also experience obstacles, disappointments, sorrow, and heartache. It's a necessary part of life, because if we had all highs and no lows, we wouldn't grow.

And unlike a fairy tale, your life isn't just one focused narrative. It's a multitude of stories, each made up of many, many chapters, all of which have their own beginnings and endings. During the difficult portions of your life, I'm asking you to believe that a favorable outcome is possible. Consider putting an end to your worry by having faith in happy endings instead of wasting your energy fretting about the worst possible outcome.

We waste far too much time worrying about things that never actually happen. That's why we're told: "Don't cross that bridge before you come to it." Believing that things can work out for the best will assist you in following this sage advice. Yet what if you keep your hopes alive but end up with a not-so-happy ending? Would focusing on the best-case scenario have been a foolish waste of time? Not at all. As I mentioned earlier, worrying wouldn't have helped or changed the outcome; no amount of anxiety will make tomorrow better. What you can do, however, is improve today by imagining the best for the times to come.

When dealing with a difficult situation, challenge your assumptions, take action to control what you can, and then let worry go. Every time I see the tiny scar on the side of my right knee or think of my mother's powerful advocacy at the hospital, I know that happy endings are indeed possible. Have faith that they'll happen for you.

Use the Worry-Free 43

Little actions make a big difference in letting go of worry. If you've done all that you can about a worrisome situation, use these "let-go" strategies.

1. Affirm the positive. Your thoughts are more powerful than you may realize. What you think, you often make happen. Experience a joy-filled and calm life by affirming the positive. For instance, instead of telling yourself that you'll never be able to let go of worry, affirm: *Letting go is simple. I easily and joyfully let go.* Instead of beating yourself up for perceived flaws, affirm: *I love and approve of myself. I am whole and perfect exactly as I am.* This does take practice, but it's certainly worth the effort. In fact, something as simple as talking to yourself in a loving, nurturing way will greatly enhance the quality of your life.

2. Aromatherapy. This holistic treatment can help calm the body and mind through the use of pleasant-smelling essential oils. Four scents believed to be quite effective in reducing anxiety and promoting relaxation are lavender, geranium, orange, and vanilla. Here are some simple ways to incorporate aromatherapy into your everyday life:

- When purchasing regular household items, such as dish soap, room deodorizer, or body wash, opt for the lavender, geranium, orange, or vanilla scents.

- Consider lighting a candle with one of those four aromas in your home or workplace.

- For the greatest mental, emotional, and spiritual impact, add a few drops of high-quality essential oil to a warm bath or massage it directly into your skin. See for yourself how something as simple as a scent can soothe a worried mind.

3. Be adventurous. When was the last time you tried something new? You could learn to ballroom dance, go rock climbing, or study a foreign language—just do something that appeals to you. Learning takes focus, but so does worry. Acquiring a new skill will help shift your focus away from your troubles and onto something productive. Not only will this help you release anxiety, it will also lead you to the kind of passion, exhilaration, and excitement that comes from being adventurous and experiencing new things.

4. Be thankful. Write a list of the things for which you're truly grateful. Focusing on them, instead of what you regret or worry about, will go a long way in building happiness and calming your mind. Spend a few moments at the beginning or end of each day to reflect on and appreciate the abundance you already possess.

5. Be yourself. Who do you think you should be: a supermom, perfect partner, power executive, or beauty queen? Is there a difference between who you *really* are and who you think you *should* be? Trying to be someone other than your true self crowds out inner peace. Don't waste time attempting to fit some other mold—just be yourself and know that you're enough!

6. Breathe. When you worry, you probably have a tendency to hold your breath or take very shallow breaths. This creates muscle tension and reduces oxygen to your brain cells. Let's face it, in the midst of worry, your brain needs all the oxygen it can get!

Stop for a moment right now and allow your mind and body to relax by taking a few slow, deep breaths. Relax your abdomen, allowing it to expand as your lower lungs fill with air. Make sure your chest and shoulders are still. (If they're moving more than your abdomen, your inhalations are too shallow.) Allow your chest and shoulders to relax, and once again, take a full, deep breath into your lower lungs.

There are several deep-breathing techniques that are quite effective. One I use regularly and find extremely beneficial is to inhale through my nose for the count of four, hold for two counts, and exhale through my mouth for another count of four. Actually counting each step momentarily takes your mind off the concerns that had you holding your breath in the first place.

Start implementing this strategy, or a similar one, into your daily routine. You'll be amazed by how relaxed, clear, and calm it can help you feel, even when the world around you seems chaotic and overwhelming.

7. "Busy" the worry out. Instead of agonizing about something you feel helpless or powerless to change, do something constructive: Play with your kids, plan your week, clean out your closet, mow your lawn, or go grocery shopping—just get busy. This will distract you from your concerns, and you'll feel better about having accomplished something other than just worrying.

8. Consume foods rich in vitamin B. In this fast-paced, fast-food world, many of us are deficient in key vitamins and minerals. When you're worried, anxious, or depressed, it may be due to a lack of vitamins B_6 and B_{12}. To ensure that you're getting enough of these powerful nutrients, consume bananas, vegetable juice, fortified whole-grain cereals, chicken, salmon, baked potatoes, eggs, spinach, and milk—all of which are good sources of vitamin B_6.

Consuming enough of vitamin B_{12} can be a little trickier, because it isn't generally present in plant products. It can, however, be found in animal products such as beef, poultry, fish, and milk. Since it's more challenging to ensure that you're getting enough of this nutrient from foods, supplements may be a good alternative. It's important to talk with a health-care professional before taking any pills or powders, because too much of any one vitamin can have dangerous side effects—but taking the right amount can be of tremendous benefit.

There are certainly other nutrients available to help you flourish physically, as well as emotionally, so do some research on your own. Visit your local library; consult a nutritionist, naturopathic doctor, or family physician; and discover for yourself how vitamins and minerals can help you "B" worry free!

9. Create a work of art. Paint, make a scrapbook, build something out of clay, or write a poem. Expressing yourself through art can induce calm and decrease worry.

10. Do what you're afraid of. Most of us are scared of something. Some women dread not fitting in, and some fear not standing out; some are terrified of failure, others of success. Everyone feels this way at one time or another. It's okay to be afraid—it's a natural emotion. However, make sure that this isn't turning into the worry that stops you from taking chances. If you aren't risking anything, you're missing out on a lot of wonderful opportunities.

If there's something in your life that you're putting on hold because fear is blocking you, erase that anxiety by doing the very thing that scares you. Your fright will diminish when you do, because you'll usually discover that what you were afraid of isn't as bad as you'd anticipated. I'm not suggesting that you take foolish risks. If you're afraid of rattlesnakes, I don't recommend jumping in front of one and offering your toe as an appetizer. However, if you've always wanted to go for a hike in the Grand Canyon, don't let your terror of reptiles stop you from following through on your dream.

By facing that specter, you can make it disappear. Conquering your fears allows you to move forward in life more easily and with less worry. See for yourself!

11. Eliminate worry-inducing words from your vocabulary. Words such as *should, can't, no one, everyone, always,* and *never* create a great deal of anxiety. Write down what you're nervous about and circle all the worry-inducing words. Then replace them with terms such as *could, prefer, can, choose not to, some people, sometimes,* and *occasionally.* Not only are these replacement words calming, they also tend to be more accurate.

12. Exercise. Do you know why you feel so good mentally after a workout? Exercise causes your brain to increase production of serotonin, a neurotransmitter that can reduce depression. In addition, it's been shown that exercise helps you *decrease* your body's cortisol levels. (Cortisol is the fat-storing hormone that your body produces when you're stressed.) As if that's not enough, there are even more benefits. Exercise has also been known to boost body image, increase self-confidence, and generate a sense of accomplishment. How long do you need to spend each week to reap these incredibly powerful benefits? Surprisingly, not much time at all. Exercising just 20 minutes, three times a week can do the trick.

If you're already working out on a regular basis, maybe it's time to try something new. The body and mind can get bored with routine, so consider breaking out of a rut with a new class (such as kickboxing, yoga, or tai chi), or a new location (such as walking outside instead of on a treadmill). It's a great way to strengthen different muscles and add excitement to your exercise regimen at the same time.

The bottom line is this: If you devote 20 minutes to exercise three times each week, you can reduce worry, enhance your body image, boost your self-confidence, and gain a sense of accomplishment. What an outstanding return on investment!

13. Focus on your accomplishments. What deeds are you most proud of? Maybe it's raising children, landing your dream job, sticking to your exercise program, raising money for a local charity, or deciding that you were going to finally do something about your worry and read this book. Taking the time to focus on what you've done can help you let go of that worried and worked-up feeling you get when focusing solely on what you haven't crossed off your list. Take a short break from all you haven't done yet in order to appreciate how far you've already come. Absorbing and celebrating your accomplishments will help you let go and find your inner calm.

14. Focus on what matters. One Saturday morning, my nine-year-old daughter, Brianna, was getting dressed to take an entrance exam at a school. Just before we left the house, I noticed that she'd matched her nice clean outfit with old sneakers. I asked, "Do you think you should put on a different pair of shoes?" She looked down at her feet and then back up at me and said, "Mom, they're not testing me on my shoes." I replied, "You're absolutely right." And we headed off to school—Brianna with her old sneakers and me with my new way of looking at them.

My daughter reminded me of something important that day: If you get too caught up in the little details, you can lose sight of what's really important. For instance, if you dwell on what you don't like about your appearance, you may lose sight of the fact you're blessed with good health. If you dwell on what you don't like in your neighborhood, you may neglect the fact that you have a nice home to live in.

As tempting as it can be, focusing solely on the little details and neglecting the bigger picture can cause a great deal of worry, stress, and dissatisfaction. How, then, can you retrain your thinking and regain satisfaction and inner peace? The remedy is to step back and ask yourself: *What really matters?* In Brianna's case, her shoes weren't really important. The test she was about to take was the main attraction. She needed to be comfortable so that she could concentrate on the exam and not worry about what was on her feet.

I'm not suggesting that you ignore *all* the details. Obviously, the little things combine to make up the bigger picture. It's important to identify areas that require some fine-tuning and take action to make positive change. I suggest, however, that you don't get so caught up that you lose sight of what's really important. Ask: *What really matters?* Allow the answer to renew your perspective and increase your inner peace.

15. Get a massage. Therapeutic massage reduces the muscle tension that worry can create and clears your mind of stressful thoughts. Where can you find a good massage therapist? Word of mouth. Ask your friends if they can recommend someone. If not, find a reputable clinic or spa in your neighborhood and book yourself for this soothing experience.

16. Give a hug. Never underestimate the healing power of touch. For a simple and quick fix to help you cope with the physical and emotional effects of worry, give someone you love a squeeze.

17. Humor your worry. Laughter causes your body to release endorphins (the body's natural painkiller) and to reduce the stress hormone cortisol. Look for ways to add humor to your life. Watch a comedy, share a funny story, or find silly photos of you and your family members—do what you can to tickle your funny bone.

18. Immerse yourself in nature. Sit or work in your garden. Lie on your back in the grass and watch the clouds go by. Take a stroll through the woods, or bundle yourself up and go for a walk in the snow. Immersing yourself in nature has an incredibly calming effect that can help you release your worries.

19. Listen to music. It's been said that "music tames the savage beast." It's true! Have you ever noticed how your favorite song can pick you up in an instant? Crank up the tunes and let the sounds melt your troubles away.

20. Meditate. Doing this for 10 to 15 minutes each day will give your body a chance to relax and provide your mind with a much-needed break from the relentless thoughts that you replay over and over again. During this time, be still and empty your mind. It can be a little tricky at first, but it *is* possible. Try focusing on instrumental music or a recording of soothing sounds, and when a thought pops into your mind, just imagine breathing it out and letting it go. Another strategy is focusing on an object, such as a painting or flower. Really concentrate on it, and if a thought pops into your mind, breathe it out and let it go again. Meditation is an invaluable tool to help you release anxiety, so make it a point to learn how.

21. Nurture yourself. Soak in the tub, enjoy a movie, have breakfast in bed, go out for dinner, snuggle under a blanket on your sofa, or read a book by the fire. Pampering yourself will push your mental "reset" button. As a working mother of two, I understand that you may think you simply don't have the time to indulge in the luxury of caring for yourself. If you feel that you're too busy, that's precisely when you need it the most!

If you've been promising to take care of yourself when you get more time, I'd like to let you in on a little secret: *You won't ever have more time—24 hours a day is all you get.* No matter who we are, what we do, or how much money we have, we all have the same amount of time allotted to us. You're going to have so much more energy and joy in those 24 hours if you put yourself first.

Does this mean that you should only take care of yourself and ignore the needs of others? Of course not, but only helping other people can end up wearing you out. Eventually, if you keep putting yourself last on the list, you won't have anything left to give. Write a "nurture-me" list and then start scheduling those activities into your calendar *before* the other commitments in your life. See for yourself how taking care of yourself first will give you the strength, stamina, and peace of mind to care for and deal with all the rest.

22. Praise yourself. Repeat after me: *I am smart, successful, intelligent, competent, creative, flexible, lovable, and beautiful.* Please feel free to add to the list! Write some powerful and positive phrases about yourself and repeat them daily. The more you believe that you're as wonderful, lovable, and deserving as you truly are, the more self-confidence and self-esteem you'll generate. On my own journey, I've found that the better I feel about myself, the more my anxiety has decreased. Shrink your own worry by increasing your confidence and self-esteem through positive self-talk—praise yourself daily!

23. Pay attention to your senses. Noticing what you see, hear, smell, taste, and touch will help you find joy in the present moment. There's tremendous power and joy available from living in the now. When you find yourself mentally borrowing trouble from the future or rehashing the past, stop and focus on the present. Pay attention to your senses: Absorb how that hug from a loved one feels, actively listen to what your friend is saying, and pay attention to the taste, texture, and aroma of each bite while you eat your next meal. Making a conscious effort to engage your senses will help you transform seemingly ordinary moments into extraordinary experiences. Stop regretting the past and worrying about the future by absorbing yourself fully in the present moment.

24. Read. From self-help to science fiction, reading expands your mind, takes you places outside of your everyday life, and gives you an escape from worrisome thoughts. When you use books specifically to let go of worry, it's important to be selective about *what* you look at. For instance, if you're releasing fear about your children being abducted, it's probably wise to avoid novels about kidnapping. On the other hand, reading a self-help book about giving your kids "street smarts" could help you craft a safety plan, and as a result, help you feel calmer. In this case, you can also consider reading a novel that has absolutely nothing to do with children so that you can escape your worried thinking for a while and give your mind a break.

When you read to regain peace, make sure that what you're putting into your mind is serving you and not working against you. Consider going to your local library or bookstore and taking home a volume that looks interesting to you. Then try reading for 15 to 30 minutes each day. See for yourself how it expands your horizons and decreases fretful thinking.

25. Record your worry. It's so easy to convince yourself that what you're upset about is going to happen, and that you'd never be able to survive if it did. Keeping a written record of what you worry about is a fantastic way to show yourself how infrequently these scenarios are actually realized. In addition, for those rare concerns that do occur, looking back on the situation and recognizing that you handled it—and are still here today—will help you build confidence in your ability to deal with anything else that may come your way. When you trust yourself, you come to see there really isn't anything you need to be frightened of, so try writing down what's bothering you.

26. Reduce caffeine. This substance can increase your blood pressure, heighten your feelings of stress and anxiety, and produce more of the stress hormone cortisol. If you're a coffee lover, as I am, this may not be the most pleasant strategy in your worry-management program, but don't despair. The good news is that you don't have to give it up altogether. Studies have shown that one or two six-ounce cups of coffee each day will have little effect on the cardiovascular system—but be careful! That third cup can end up increasing your worry, stress, and anxiety levels. If you want to calm your mind, gradually reduce your caffeine intake.

27. Relax your jaw. Take a moment right now to release those muscles and allow your mouth to open naturally with the pull of gravity. What do you notice? Did your entire body follow suit and relax as well? An important part of letting go of worry is to release the muscle tension that it creates. When you need a quick fix to help with this process, close your eyes and focus your attention on relaxing your jaw. You'll be amazed by how much more calm you'll feel after only 60 seconds.

28. Rock. The motion of swaying back and forth can calm your body and mind. As women, we instinctively know the soothing effects of this motion, since it's something we automatically do to comfort a crying baby. Both my daughters had colic when they were babies. During those periods in my life, I think the rocking was more to calm me than the infants! One of the best parts of this technique is that it's free, and you can do it anywhere. The next time worry hits, try rocking your concerns away.

29. Say no. It's imperative that you don't take on more commitments than you can reasonably handle. Being overstressed from having too much on your plate can often result in more negative thoughts, assumptions, and feelings—the perfect conditions for worry to grow.

Learn to say no when you've reached your limit. It can be challenging to decline requests, especially if you're a people pleaser. Believe me, I've been there and understand how it feels. Here are three worry-free ways I've found to turn people down politely:

1. *Thank and decline:* "I appreciate your asking me to volunteer. Regrettably, I'm unavailable to help this time."

2. *Compliment and decline:* "Your party sounds like fun; however, I'm unable to attend."

3. *Best wishes and decline:* "I wish you much success with your event. Unfortunately, I'm unable to participate this year."

I'm not suggesting that you reject all offers or requests—after all, helping is important, as is getting together with friends and loved ones. I'm simply saying that if you're reaching (or have already reached) your limit, you should acknowledge that fact and say no to protect your own well-being and regain your inner calm.

30. Schedule "worry time." Give yourself 10 to 15 minutes each day to fret. During this period, write in a journal, make an action plan, or call a friend to vent, but don't allow yourself to go over the allotted limit. When the time is up, end the session, and consciously focus on another subject, or better yet, physically get up and do something else. If an anxious thought pops up outside of your scheduled worry time, simply add it to a "think-about-it-later" list and move on.

This is an unconventional strategy, but here's why it works: As silly as it sounds, you may replay your worries over and over again because you're afraid that you'll forget about them. When you write down your concerns and have a scheduled appointment for dealing with them, you're able to rest assured that you'll remember them.

Try this technique and you'll discover that something amazing happens. When your set "worry time" comes, you might not even feel like agonizing over everything on your list! Even if you do, you'll have the time you need to vent your concerns, which plays a major role in letting them go. Remember, when your "worry time" is up—move on.

31. Set a date to do something you love. Rather than spending your days worrying about the future, plan events that you can look forward to. From something as simple as a dinner out at your favorite restaurant to something as elaborate as an exotic vacation, this fun and simple strategy will help you transform fearful apprehension into excited anticipation.

32. Sleep well. Rest plays a significant role in vitality and well-being, and experts agree that most people need on average of six to eight hours each night. How much do you need? As mentioned in a previous chapter, let your body be your guide. If you wake up rested, you're probably okay.

However, be careful that you're not overdoing it, since getting too much shut-eye can actually make you feel more fatigued during the day. In some cases, oversleeping can be a sign of an underlying medical condition, in which case you may want to speak with your physician.

You may also want to talk with your health-care provider or naturopathic doctor if you're suffering from insomnia. There are holistic treatments that can help you overcome this hurdle and get the sleep you require. Do what you can to get a good night's rest and calm your tired, worried mind.

33. Slow down. You probably tend to race around when you're worried and overwhelmed—your mind starts racing, and your body follows suit. During these times, slow down your movements. If you're walking, reduce your strides. If you're driving, make sure you're not speeding; if you are, take your foot off the gas and stay within the speed limit. If you're talking, establish a more relaxed pace. By consciously slowing down your movements, your mind will relax, too. And as your thoughts decelerate, you'll feel calmer and a lot less frazzled.

34. Spend time with a pet. Animal companions can help reduce worry in several ways:

- They can help reduce your feelings of loneliness, which is one of those emotions that's likely to cause a return to negative behavior patterns (such as making negative assumptions that lead to worry).

- You can confide in a pet and never worry about being judged.

- Some pets can even help you worry less about being a victim of a crime. I know I feel safe with my two massive German shepherds on the alert.

While there are many benefits of having a pet, it's important to make sure that the type you decide to bring into your life works with your personality and living space so that you reduce your worry rather than adding to it! If you can't have a furry friend in your home, consider volunteering your time at local animal shelter. It's a great way to help your community and benefit from a little anxiety-reducing therapy at the same time.

35. Spend time with positive people. I've found time and time again that when you spend time with negative people, you end up feeling negative, and vice versa. It makes sense, then, to hang out with positive people in order to help let go of worry. If you don't have a strong social network of upbeat acquaintances to connect with, consider joining a group to increase your circle of friends. Volunteering your time on a fund-raising committee is a good way to meet new people and help others at the same time. Taking a night-school class is an excellent way to expand your social base and your skills in the process. Enjoy cultivating new and rewarding relationships while you're involved in a fun activity. As you spend time with positive people, you'll find that their hope and optimism can help you clear up negative thinking.

36. Spread it out. Piling all your worries into one mental lump can cause a great deal of internal anguish. The key to regaining your peace of mind is to spread it out. Just as you wouldn't try to eat an entire week's worth of food in one sitting, avoid trying to tackle a lifetime of fears all at once. Instead, write down your concerns on paper and work through the CALM process in baby steps. Shifting your thinking to a one-worry-at-a-time mentality will put you in a much better position to take action on those things that are within your control and to let go of those that aren't.

37. Step into the light. It's common to feel down and worry more during the winter months when your exposure to the sun is reduced. To combat these blues, get as much light as you can. Keep your environment bright (with natural illumination, as much as possible), participate in outdoor activities, and talk to your doctor about other light-therapy options. Increasing your exposure to natural, outdoor light will enhance your mood, leaving less mental space for worry.

38. Talk to a friend. This will give you the opportunity to vent your concerns, and in many cases, you may receive some positive feedback or creative solutions that will help you stop fretting.

39. Trust yourself. Are you worried about something over which you have no control? Trust yourself and let it go. You've already handled everything that life has dealt to you, and you'll be able to take care of whatever else comes your way. Affirm: *I have the skills I need to solve problems. I have survived and thrived beyond challenges in the past, and I trust that if the need arises, I can do it again.*

40. Turn off the news. Give yourself the gift of turning off these horrific sights and sounds. They can shock your body to the core and give you things to worry about that you hadn't even thought of before. If you're a regular news watcher, cutting out this ritual will free up some of your time. During this newfound break, take in some comforting images: Walk by a park and listen to children's laughter or sit outside with loved ones and watch the sun set. Participating in *your* life rather than watching others' lives in the news will help soothe your mind and reconnect you with the inner peace that worry crowds out.

41. Visualize success. If there's something you want in your life, visualize it. If you long to be free from worry, envision everything turning out the way you want it to, rather than focusing on what could go wrong. If you're anxious about an upcoming event, see it turning out exactly as you hope. Mentally picturing your desired outcome builds confidence, which leads to improved performance. In this way, your vision becomes a self-fulfilling prophecy.

If you want to achieve a greater level of fitness, visualize yourself exercising with a strong and lean body. If you want a new home, instead of mentally telling yourself that it's not possible, picture your dream house in your mind. What does it look like? Where is it? See yourself in it.

Keep in mind that this technique doesn't replace action. To accomplish anything in life, you must do something. However, visualization is the fuel that will help you believe that the action is worth taking. This week, see your success, because when you believe you can achieve, you most certainly can.

42. Volunteer. Giving your time to help someone in need will make you feel good about yourself, and will make it easier for you to put your own problems into perspective. When you help others, you end up helping yourself.

43. Walk. If your emotional batteries need recharging, go for a stroll. The fresh air, sunlight, and exercise—and the good feelings you get from doing something healthy for yourself—will significantly improve your mood!

In this chapter, you've learned 52 strategies that will help you let go of the uncontrollable—and now it's time to begin incorporating them into your life. As I mentioned earlier, there are two ways you can do so. The first method is to choose the techniques that seem most appealing to you. If this is the direction you'd like to take, go back and circle five of your favorites. Then when worry hits, pick one of your "top five" to help you let go. After you've used each of them, it's a good idea to go back and give some of the other the ideas a shot. Even those that may seem a little unusual will go a long way in helping you kick the worry habit.

The second method is to implement one new strategy each week for 52 weeks. If this is the route you prefer, begin working your way through the choices as they appear in this chapter. As you make your way down the list, draw a star beside the ones that work best for you. When worries arise in the future, you'll be able to quickly refer back to what helped you the most.

While you're letting go of the uncontrollable, continue acting to control the controllable and challenge your assumptions. In addition, add the fourth step of the CALM process to the mix, and master your mind.

Chapter Four

Introduction

Transform yourself from a worrier into a warrior.

The fourth step in the CALM process is to master your mind. It's here that you'll discover how to guard against your own negative thinking. You'll learn how to put an end to destructive mental chatter and adopt a positive inner dialogue, and in doing so, transform yourself from a worrier into a warrior.

What does it mean to be a warrior? In the context of this book, it means to reclaim your personal power by taking control of your thinking and choosing where you focus your attention. This may sound like a tall order; however, take a close look at the words *worrier* and *warrior.* Notice that the shift from one to the other is simply two letters. Sometimes even a dramatic change is accomplished with only a small modification, and you can make a dramatic transformation from a worrier into a warrior with a simple shift in the way you talk to yourself.

We all talk to ourselves on a regular basis, and there are two extremes in how we do this. On one end of the spectrum is abusive self-talk. If you tend to do this, you'll probably notice that you're quite hard on yourself. You may beat yourself up over every perceived flaw and imperfection and have many limiting beliefs about what you are or aren't capable of accomplishing. Perhaps you carry around a great deal of guilt, feel sorry for yourself, or believe that you're just not good enough. When you make mistakes, you probably torture yourself with thoughts such as: *What's wrong with me? Why do I always make mistakes? I can never do anything right.*

At the other extreme is nurturing self-talk. If you tend to do this, you'll likely notice that you recover easily from setbacks and focus more on your strengths than your weaknesses. You probably have high self-confidence and self-worth, along with an inner awareness that no matter what you've done (or not done), you're good enough just the way you are. You often choose to learn from your mistakes and let them go, instead of beating yourself up over them. In fact, when you mess up, you probably boost yourself up with thoughts such as: *That's okay; we all make mistakes. I'll learn from it and do better next time.*

My all-time favorite example of nurturing self-talk occurred when I attended a full-day seminar that a colleague was giving. After her session concluded, I walked up to the front of the room to talk with her. While we were in the middle of our conversation, a man who'd been in the audience came up and asked her if she was pregnant. She told him that she was *not*. After he left, she turned to me, and with a look of complete disbelief on her face, said, "That's the strangest pickup line I have ever heard!"

How's that for nurturing self-talk? How would you have responded in that situation? Would you have thought you were being hit on? Or would you have said to yourself, *I'm going to go home, burn this outfit, and never eat again!* The latter would show a tendency toward abusive self-talk.

Which extreme do you more closely relate to? Is your inner dialogue more loving, or is it often harsh? It's imperative to be conscious of how you speak to yourself, because it's your internal dialogue that largely dictates whether you feel worried or calm—you can talk yourself into feeling anxious or relaxed.

In addition, when you stop and really become aware of what you're telling yourself in any given situation, you assume a position of personal power. You're able to identify those occasions when you're slipping toward the abusive end of the scale (and we all do that from time to time). As a result of your awareness, you're able to do something about it. You have the ability to get out of the negative loop and move your self-talk to the nurturing end of the spectrum.

This chapter presents 11 strategies that will help you shift your inner dialogue so that you can begin speaking to yourself in a nurturing way on a regular basis. You'll notice that each section begins with a *worrier* thought and three replacement *warrior* thoughts. The former represent abusive self-talk; these are some of the common viewpoints and self-limiting beliefs that block many women from enjoying inner peace. The latter represent nurturing self-talk; these are the statements, beliefs, and in some cases, questions that you can use as replacements. The new, empowering thoughts will help you build self-belief, self-confidence, and self-worth. They'll assist you in putting an end to "What-if" thinking. You'll begin to regain hope and excitement for life and release both the guilt and the judgments that erode your inner peace.

The time has come to take back your personal power, to take control of your thinking, and to choose where you focus your thoughts. Now is the time for you to turn yourself from a worrier into a warrior—so let the transformation begin.

Accept Responsibility

The *worrier* says: "It's not my fault that I worry."

The *warrior* says: "Worry is a choice."
                    "I choose to let go of worry."
                    "I intend to live with inner peace."

There was a time when I was convinced that my weight was the source of my worry. Despite well-meaning advice from friends and family, I thought if I could only lose enough weight, my troubles would disappear. I believed that being thin would fix everything: Everyone would like me, I'd love myself, and I'd finally be calm and carefree.

Perhaps that belief stemmed from being "the chubby kid" in elementary school. I was teased terribly about my weight as a child, and I used humor to hide my pain until I was about 14 years old. That's when I exchanged my class-clown routine for starvation—I'd go days without eating. I lost weight, and the teasing from my peers ceased, but my world still wasn't worry free. To me, that continued anxiety simply meant that I wasn't thin enough. So I continued to starve myself on and off until I was 16 years old.

At that age, I exchanged starvation for bulimia. The disorder consumed me, and I was repulsed by it. Yet I still believed that when I was thin enough, everything would be okay—but I was wrong. In fact, the thinner I became, the more messed up and anxiety-ridden I felt. At the age of 17, I was at the end of my rope, and I booked an appointment with a psychologist to begin the slow and steady process of overcoming my eating disorders and getting my life back on track.

The reason I'm sharing this very personal story is to let you know that I understand how it feels to believe: *If only I could lose this weight, then I wouldn't have to worry. If I only had more money, then I could relax. If I only had a better job, then everything would be okay.* Let me tell you, if you don't have calm without those things, you won't have it with them, either. You'll just find something else to stress about. I know because I've been there and experienced both sides of the coin. I've been broke and had money, had some great jobs as well as some pretty lousy ones. I've been too heavy and at my ideal weight.

Through it all, I've learned this very important truth: Money, weight, children, parents, workload, health, career, and other people don't make you worry. Do you know what makes you upset? *You* do. But that's actually great news, because it means that you don't have to win the lottery, shed pounds, find a mate, get a divorce, change jobs, or fix whatever else it is that you've been blaming in order to regain inner calm. What you do need to do is accept responsibility for your anxiety and stop associating it with external factors.

Accepting responsibility doesn't mean that you condemn yourself—all that does is move you from externalizing your worry to internalizing it. It's not about whose *fault* it is. Instead, it's about empowering yourself to make positive changes in your life, accepting responsibility, and taking back your personal strength. Affirm: *Worry is a choice. I choose to let go of worry. I intend to live with peace of mind.* Then move on to the next "Master Your Mind" strategy.

Challenge Limiting Beliefs

The *worrier* says: "I'm not okay."

The *warrior* says: "I am okay exactly as I am."
                      "I am special exactly as I am."
                      "I am valuable exactly as I am."

When my daughter Brianna was in the third grade, she was given a homework assignment on facts and opinions. It was a page of about 20 statements, and her task was to determine whether each one was a fact or an opinion. Here are four of the sentences, along with her answers:

- Some families have dogs as pets. *Fact*
- Dogs are better pets than cats. *Opinion*
- Apples grow on trees. *Fact*
- A banana tastes disgusting. *Fact*

In reviewing her work, I noticed that she'd made a mistake with the last answer. I said, "Brianna, you said it's a fact that a banana tastes disgusting, but I ate one for breakfast today. So, is it a fact or an opinion?" She replied, "It's a fact that you ate a disgusting banana for breakfast today!" As she spoke, I realized that some of the beliefs we hang on to—even those that do more harm than good—are opinions, yet we live our lives as though they're facts.

As mentioned previously, one of the beliefs I struggled with for many years was: "I'm not okay *now*, but if I could just lose ten more pounds, *then* I'd be lovable, valuable, and attractive." I never challenged that idea; I just accepted it as a fact. I'm sure that many of you are struggling with this same assumption, and if you are, it's time to challenge it. Is it a *fact* or an *opinion* that you're not okay now, but if you lost 10, 20, or 30 pounds, then you'd finally be lovable, valuable, and attractive? I know that you may be chuckling right now, emphatically shouting, "Fact!" However, I guarantee you that this is an opinion. The fact is that if you lost ten pounds, you'd be a little lighter—not more lovable, a better person, or more valuable as a human being. Those are all matters of opinion.

I'm not suggesting that opinions are unimportant or that you should discard your preferences and the thoughts of others. By all means, have opinions—keep, share, contemplate, change, and *challenge* them. I do believe that you need to be mindful in order to avoid blindly mistaking opinion for fact. Too many of us carry around the pain of past criticisms, rejection, and put-downs because we've made this error. Too many of us torture ourselves with weight worries and live with low self-esteem because we've believed that a particular sentiment is factual.

Opinions aren't facts. The latter tell only that which is true or can be proven true. The former, on the other hand, aren't founded on certainty or proof—although some of these beliefs are important to keep. They may inspire you to reach incredible heights and overcome enormous obstacles. Hang on to concepts that encourage you, build your self-esteem, and increase your inner peace.

On the flip side, some of these ideas tear at the very core of your self-worth. They may make you feel that you're not acceptable, lovable, worthy, capable, or valuable. These are the ones that must be challenged—don't just accept them. Question the validity of each one of your limiting beliefs by asking: "Is it a fact or an opinion?" More often than not, you'll discover that it isn't really true. Consciously distinguishing between the two will help you let go of that which no longer serves you.

Become aware of your own beliefs. Do they make you feel better or worse? Do they help or harm? Are they fact or opinion? Are they your opinions or someone else's? Now is the time to challenge all the assumptions that limit you, hurt you, and steal your peace. Fill your life with facts and opinions that build you up, create joy, and inspire greatness. That is, decide whether bananas are "disgusting" to you—and if you think that they're tasty, then enjoy every bite.

Balance Negative Labels

The *worrier* says: "I'm such a worrywart."

The *warrior* says: "I'm calm."
"I'm confident about the future."
"I'm a warrior."

What words do you use to describe yourself? Do you mostly see yourself as: calm, strong, confident, lovable, deserving, smart, competent, successful, brave, beautiful, and other empowering, positive words? Or, do you mostly use negative labels, such as: bad, damaged, failure, flawed, incompetent, stupid, lazy, undeserving, selfish, and worrywart? It's important to be aware of the words that you use to describe yourself because you become what you consistently tell yourself that you are.

Your mind will do its best to prove you right. For instance, if you tell yourself that you're a failure who can never stick to a diet, you might subconsciously (or consciously) blow your healthy-eating plan to show that you're right. If you say that you're incompetent, you'll likely dwell on your mistakes instead of your accomplishments, and perhaps even subconsciously trip yourself up to confirm your beliefs are accurate. If you call yourself a hopeless worrywart, you may decide to abandon the CALM process in order to prove to yourself that your label is correct.

Because you're an achiever, competent, and deserving of all that you desire, you'll be successful in your attempts—and you'll be able to continue worrying. In essence, the negative labels you give yourself become self-fulfilling prophecies. The good news is that you can get out of this loop with the following steps:

— **Identify the labels you use to describe yourself.** Write down as many words as possible to complete the statement: "I am . . ." Record whatever words pop into your mind, and continue adding to the list until you feel that you've captured the majority of the labels you consistently use to tell yourself who you are.

— **Understand that we're all both positive and negative.** Once your list is complete, take a look at the words you've written down with the understanding that we're not good *or* bad, strong *or* weak, and perfect *or* flawed. Instead, we're good *and* bad, strong *and* weak, and perfect *and* flawed. This insight will go a long way in helping you increase your self-confidence and self-esteem. You won't let your labels affect how you feel about yourself because you'll know that they aren't the entire story. As a result, you won't get hooked into believing solely in the negative descriptions and allowing them to dominate your thoughts to the point where they become self-fulfilling prophecies.

— **Balance out the negative labels.** The final step is to offset each harsh judgment with at least three positive labels. Here are three examples:

1. The *worrier* says: "I'm broken."
    The *warrior* says: "I'm whole. I'm complete. I'm beautiful."

2. The *worrier* says: "I'm bad."
    The *warrior* says: "I'm good. I'm lovable. I'm kind."

3. The *worrier* says: "I'm undeserving."
    The *warrior* says: "I'm deserving. I'm equal. I'm unique."

Why do you need three positive labels? Unfortunately, the negative ones have likely been ingrained in your mind for many, many years, so they can seem more believable than the uplifting ones. Balancing the scale with at least three loving statements can make the process of shifting your beliefs a little easier.

Try it yourself: Identify labels that you use to describe yourself. Understand that you're both positive and negative, and balance out unpleasant beliefs with at least three nurturing statements about who you are. When you tip the scale in this way, something amazing happens. Just as you looked for opportunities to prove that you were right about the negative labels, you'll also work to show that you're right about the positive ones. Once again, what you tell yourself you are, you become. Only this time, what you turn into is a more peaceful, more powerful, and happier you.

Catch and Correct
All-or-Nothing Thinking

The *worrier* says: *"Everything always* ends
up a complete disaster."

The *warrior* says: *"Sometimes* things
don't turn out as planned."

"Things are seldom as bad
as they seem."

"I can choose to make the best
of this situation."

"We'll *never* make it! Why do things like this *always* happen to me? It's a *complete* disaster!" Most of us have used these types of all-or-nothing statements at one time or another. Back when I was a worrier, such thoughts had me trapped in a whirlwind of worry. At 1:30 one afternoon, my husband, my two daughters, and I were caught on the highway in the middle of a snowstorm. Blizzards don't usually bother me, but we grown-ups were on our way to begin a vacation in Saint Lucia—and I was *positive* that we were going to miss our flight.

Earlier that day, the sun had been shining brightly, and it looked as if we were going to have an uneventful trip to the airport. All we had to do was drive our daughters to my husband's parents' house, where they'd be spending the week. My in-laws lived 90 minutes east of our home, and the airport was a one-hour drive west of our place. So we figured that if we left at 1 P.M., we'd be able to drop off the kids and arrive at the airport hotel with plenty of time to enjoy a nice leisurely dinner and hit the sack early enough to wake refreshed for our 6 A.M. flight. But there we were, only 30 minutes into the drive, and it was snowing so hard that we could barely see the road.

After three hours of inching along the snow-covered streets, we arrived at the country lane that my in-laws lived on, but their house was a half-mile down the road, and there was no way our van would make it through the snow. My husband called his dad, who suggested that we drive to his friend's car dealership in town and borrow one of the trucks, so we did. We piled the kids and their luggage into the borrowed truck, left our van at the dealership, and headed back to my in-laws' place.

Once again, we reached the snowy country lane, and my husband said, "We have no other choice but to gun it." He put the pedal to the metal, I crossed my fingers, and we proceeded to hydroplane up onto the snow—so much so that the tires weren't even touching the surface of the road. We were officially stuck, and I started to whine, "Oh, that's just great! Our *entire* vacation is ruined."

While lamenting our situation, I noticed some neighborhood teens driving around on snowmobiles. I waved them over and asked if they'd take us by snowmobile to my in-laws' house. Happy to help, they began shuttling me, my husband, our daughters, and the girls' luggage to my in-laws' place. It was now 6 P.M., the time we'd originally planned on arriving at the airport hotel.

The teens took my husband and me back to the borrowed truck by snowmobile and pushed us onto the main street. We drove back into town, returned the truck, hopped into our van, and began the slow and snowy journey to the airport. I was sure that we'd *never* make it. Over and over again, I replayed thoughts of how terrible it was that we'd wasted all that money on a trip we wouldn't be able to take. I felt sorry for myself and wondered why things like that *always* happened to me. I was convinced that it was a complete disaster.

Have you ever done something similar—gotten yourself all worked up by exaggerating a situation and blowing it out of proportion? If so, you'll be happy to know that there's a way to regain your composure and calm your mind, even when it feels as though everything is ruined.

The first step is to catch your all-or-nothing thinking, and the best way to accomplish this is to capture your thoughts on paper. Write down exactly what you're telling yourself. In my case, some of the key phrases were: *We'll never make it! Why do things like this always happen to me? It's a complete disaster!* Maybe you're telling yourself: *I always make mistakes. No one appreciates me. I can't trust anybody.* Whatever it is, identify it in writing.

The second step is to replace the phrases with more accurate truths. Consider: *I make some mistakes, and I also do many things right. It's safe for me to make errors, and I can learn from them. Some people appreciate me, and I appreciate myself. I'm trustworthy, and many others are, too.* Do you think that these new phrases might help you regain your inner calm and stop your thinking from spiraling out of control? Sure they would!

Imagine if I'd replaced my own all-or-nothing self-talk with more accurate truths such as: *I'm not sure we're going to make it to the airport in time for our flight. However, we're still moving forward right now, and we're doing the best we can. It's true that I've had a few travel snags in the past, and I'm not sure we'll make it to the airport in time for our flight. I hope we do, but if we don't, it won't be the end of the world.* Do you suppose that would have helped restore my peace of mind? Of course! In addition, the replacement thoughts make much more sense because they're far more accurate.

The exaggerations we conjure up are seldom correct. My trip to the airport on that snowy winter's day is an example. Yes, we were delayed. In fact, we arrived at the airport hotel (where, incidentally, not a flake of snow had fallen!) at 1 A.M. the next morning, which still provided us with the benefit of a few hours of sleep before our flight. We showed up at the airport, and without a hitch, our plane took off with us on it. The only disaster was the one I'd created in my mind while I was whining in the blizzard.

This new habit of talking to yourself in a more accurate and truthful way will help you calm your mind. It's certainly helped me move beyond my own "Why-do-things-like-this-*always*-happen-to-me?" days. In fact, while writing this book, my husband and I had a conference to attend in Orlando. We were really looking forward to the trip, but the weather reports indicated a category-4 hurricane would be hitting Florida the day of our departure.

Using the concept of catching and correcting all-or-nothing thinking, I was able to prevent anxiety from creeping in. Rather than stressing about the situation and making it worse for myself than it really was, I created Plan B. I said to my husband, "The kids are looked after for the week, so if we can't fly to Orlando, let's go somewhere else. Let's use the week and make the best of it."

Not only did this positive self-talk calm my mind and prevent worry from rearing its ugly head, it got me excited about the possibility of taking a spur-of-the-moment trip to an unplanned destination. In the end, we were able to fly into Orlando with only a three-hour weather delay, and throughout the ordeal, I retained my peace of mind.

Develop the habit of catching and correcting your all-or-nothing thinking. Using accurate truths to describe your situation will help you replace feelings of utter despair with peace and hope. It may take a little time and effort to acquire this skill, but it will be worth it.

Avoid Feeling Sorry for Yourself

The *worrier* says: "Poor me."

The *warrior* says: "I trust that every experience serves me."

"I have faith in the process of life."

"I am at peace."

You looked forward to your tropical vacation all year, but it rained the entire trip. You stuck to your diet and exercise program all week, but gained two pounds. You finally landed the job of your dreams, but were laid off a month later.

Life has many unexpected twists and turns. When those unpredicted events fall short of your high expectations, it's very easy to feel angry, hurt, and frustrated. Is it wrong to be upset when things don't turn out as you anticipated? Of course not. Acknowledge your disappointment and allow yourself to feel angry, to cry, and to vent . . . just not for too long.

You want to avoid holding on to upset feelings for an excessive length of time, because if you don't release them, you'll lose too much precious time. Every minute that you spend upset, you lose a minute of happiness. Anger means lost harmony, and worry sacrifices peace. It's your life, and they're your moments. How you spend your time isn't determined by circumstance, it's up to you—you're the one who chooses how you feel.

I understand that making these choices can sometimes seem like an impossible task, especially when something we view as unfair has happened. I was reminded of just how challenging it can be when I attempted to withdraw money from an ATM in Dallas. I swiped my debit card down the side of the machine, entered my PIN, and punched in the withdrawal amount of $200. Right after I pushed the *Enter* button, the message on the screen read: "Transaction in process." After waiting for what seemed to be an unusually long time, a new message appeared. It read: "Financial institution not recognized. Terminal shutting down." The screen went black. I stood there for a few minutes to see if it would come back online, but it didn't, so I walked away in search of another bank machine.

Two days later, as I balanced my account online, I discovered that the original ATM had in fact withdrawn the money from my account—*plus* the U.S.-Canadian exchange rate and a hefty processing fee—even though I didn't get any cash! I immediately called my bank to explain what had happened. The customer-service representative I spoke to said that someone would look into it, but since it was an independent bank machine, I probably wouldn't be getting my money back. I was mad! I wasn't angry at my financial institution, but rather at the owners of the faulty ATM who walked away scot-free with my money.

Yes, unfair things happen. When they do, by all means acknowledge your feelings—and then choose to move on. This second part is crucial. You must go forward, otherwise you'll likely end up feeling sorry for yourself, which won't serve you well. In fact, when you indulge in self-pity, you transform yourself into a victim and give your personal power away; you move from being power*ful* to power*less*.

Feeling helpless creates a great deal of worry, because you're likely to fret about things that you feel you have no control over. Ultimately, choosing to feel sorry for yourself is choosing to give away control and peace of mind. That said, it's important to understand that we'll all have our "poor-me" moments from time to time. We're human, after all. What's important is that you recognize your self-pity, then choose to regain your personal power and move on.

How do you go about this? One strategy is to rewrite the scenario. In other words, make up a more satisfying ending to the story. Here's the conclusion that I created to help me release my anger and "poor-me" thinking: I imagined that after I walked away from the ATM, the cash did pop out. At that exact moment, a single mother who was struggling to make ends meet walked by and found it. The relief and joy I imagined that she felt began to melt away my anger, and I started to feel much better.

At first glance, rewriting the scenario may seem like nothing more than foolish thinking. But which is more ridiculous: holding on to unproductive rage or doing what you can to let it go—even if that means using your imagination to create a more palatable story? This exercise won't change an unfair thing, and it doesn't mean that you approve of what's happened. By all means, when something unfair occurs, examine it carefully. If you discover a problem that needs to be solved, do what you can to bring about justice. Change what needs to be changed, and learn what needs to be learned (in my case, I decided to avoid using independent ATMs). Then let it go.

Another way to retain your personal power and inner peace when life throws you a curveball is to choose to believe that each new experience ultimately serves you in a positive way. I personally believe that everything that happens to me serves a purpose. Yet I have to confess that when the experience is an unpleasant one, finding the benefit behind it can be tough. Take, for instance, the unpleasant encounter I had back when I first set out to find a full-time job. I'd been offered a six-week position at an insurance company, covering for a woman who was away on medical leave. I jumped at the opportunity because I was having a tough time finding work, and it turned out to be a good move. I enjoyed the job—and the much-needed paycheck—so much so that when it was time to go, I was quite sad.

The woman for whom I'd been covering phoned me a few weeks after I'd left and asked if I knew where a certain client file was. It was a really weird question, since I hadn't been there for weeks. I told her I didn't know where it was, and she thanked me and hung up. A few months later, I ran into the company manager at the mall. We stopped to chat, and I told him the good news that I'd landed a permanent position with a financial-planning firm. He said, "That must be why you didn't accept our job offer."

Confused, I asked, "What job offer?" He explained that the woman for whom I'd been covering had decided to quit, and he'd asked her to phone me to see if I'd like to replace her on a permanent basis. At that point, I was more baffled than ever. Had she asked me that strange question so that she could "truthfully" tell the manager that she'd called me? Why hadn't she offered me the job? Trying to figure out "why" consumed more of my time and energy than I care to admit, but eventually I stopped trying to understand it and got on with my life—until now.

Today—18 years later and with the advantage of hindsight—I began pondering the question again. I asked myself, *What could be the <u>positive</u> reason behind my encounter with the woman at the insurance company?* The answer hit me like a ton of bricks: If she'd offered me the job, I would have accepted. I wouldn't have found a position with the financial-planning company, where I met my husband, with whom I've had two beautiful daughters. In addition, the company I ended up working for *paid* me to learn presentation skills and sent me to a seminar where I met someone who mentored me on the path to becoming a professional speaker. If that woman at the insurance company had offered me the job, I would have missed out on the life I have now.

Has an unpleasant encounter or situation ended up serving you in a positive way? For instance, did it cause you to become a stronger or more knowledgeable person? Did it inspire you to make a difference in the lives of others? Did it teach you something or give you an experience that you might have otherwise missed? The more you search for the positive reason behind each event, the easier the unpleasant encounters are to bear. If you're unable to find anything good, have faith in the process of life and trust that each new experience benefits you. This will allow you to retain your personal power and your peace of mind.

The next time you're faced with one of life's unexpected twists and turns, acknowledge your feelings and then move on. Try rewriting the scenario and trust that everything ultimately serves you in a positive way. Often, the experiences that were the most difficult to bear end up being the very best things that could have happened. As for that woman at the insurance company many years ago, I just have one thing to say: *Thank you!*

Release Guilt

The *worrier* says: "I should/shouldn't have."

The *warrior* says: "I'm doing the best I can,
and my best is enough."

"I'm doing what is appropriate
in this situation."

"I can choose to take action
and make positive changes."

One day near the beginning of the school year, I'd just reminded my then-eight-year-old daughter to pack her dance clothes in her school bag. Obviously not thrilled with the request, she let out a big sigh and said, "Mom, why do I *always* have to pack my own bag? *All* of the other kids' moms *always* pack their kids' bags."

Ah, the guilt trip. There was a time when her strategy might have worked. It used to be that my internal dialogue would have gone something like this: *If I were a good mom, I would pack my kids' bags like all the other moms do.* Then I would have either made a mad dash to pack her things, or at the very least, beat myself up for the rest of the day for not being as good as the other mothers. But times have changed, baby, and if I'm packing any bags, it certainly won't be to take a guilt trip!

Most of us have experienced guilt at one time or another. I'm not talking about the feeling you might get from breaking the law or committing a crime. I mean your agony when you can't be there for your children, family, or partner; that "tied-up-in-knots" feeling that comes when you say no to someone else and yes to yourself; and the shame that stems from not allowing yourself the right to be human. If you've ever been gripped by such emotions, this section contains what you need to know to move from feeling guilt-y to guilt-free.

Challenge Guilt-Trigger Words

Words such as *always* and *never* are guilt triggers, and as I mentioned earlier, they're seldom accurate. My daughter's response to my request was loaded with these terms, and I called her on it. I said, "I really doubt that *all* the other mothers *always* pack their kids' bags. Besides, you don't *always* pack your own bag."

Another guilt-trigger word to watch out for is *should*—this one is high impact. For instance, there are many women working outside the home who feel guilty because they think that they *should* be staying with their kids, and many stay-at-home moms feel bad because they think that they *should* be contributing more to the family's income. Worn-out women aren't okay with relaxing because they think that they *should* be busy working on something else. Can you see how much worry a little word can create? To challenge guilt-trigger words, ask yourself:

— **"Is the statement I'm hearing or the belief I'm holding 100 percent accurate?"** This question will help remind you to catch and correct these upsetting terms, providing you with the perspective you need to free yourself from guilty feelings. Write down what you're feeling bad about and then circle each guilt-trigger word. Rewrite your emotions in a more accurate light, eliminating everything that you circled.

Release Self-Judgment

Guilt stems from judging your choices as good or bad. When we think we've made the wrong choice, we feel guilty, but the trouble is that life isn't black or white. There are many shades of gray, so it's not as simple as "good or bad." To release self-judgment, ask yourself a more sophisticated set of questions. Here are two for you to try:

1. "Am I doing the best I can?" So you're feeling guilty because you had to work late, the house isn't as clean as you think it *should* be, the grass hasn't been cut, you ate that second piece of pie, or you were short with the kids at breakfast. There's no use beating yourself up over it. What's done is done, and nobody's perfect, so don't demand perfection from yourself. You can only do your best. *Try your best, and let go of the rest.*

2. "Is what I'm doing appropriate in this situation?" Was it appropriate for me to have my daughter pack her school bag? Of course it was. In fact, it went beyond that and taught her about responsibility and contributing to the family.

Is it appropriate to order dinner in instead of making it yourself when you have to work late? Of course it is. Is it fitting for you to take time to relax when you're feeling worn-out, even if there are e-mails to be answered and phone calls to be returned? Absolutely. In fact, when you take time to recharge your batteries, you'll discover that you're more productive than you are when you push yourself to exhaustion.

However, there may be times when those two questions reveal that what you're doing isn't appropriate or that you're not doing your best. Should you feel guilty then? Absolutely not. Self-reproach isn't productive, but creating an action plan is.

Create an Action Plan

An action plan is your list of strategies for making positive changes, resolving problems, and learning from past mistakes. To create your own, ask yourself these two questions:

1. "What actions can I take to make this situation more favorable?" Become an active participant in making a change for the better. For instance, if you're feeling guilty about working long hours instead of spending time with your family or friends, create an action plan that includes specific dates and times when you'll be together. Not only does this help reduce your worry while you're working, it also gives you something to look forward to.

2. "What did I learn from this, and what will I do differently next time?" Sometimes the best we can do is to acknowledge we've made a mistake, learn from it, and move on. When you acquire wisdom from your experiences and make the conscious decision to modify your future behavior, it helps prevent you from repeating the guilt-producing action.

Freedom from guilt is the opportunity to live, take chances, make mistakes, and experience inner peace. You deserve that, and it all begins with one small shift in what you ask yourself each and every day. If you've been feeling guilty, change your questions and ask: *Is the statement I'm hearing or the belief I'm holding 100 percent accurate? Am I doing the best I can? Is what I'm doing appropriate in this instance? What actions can I take to make this situation more favorable? What did I learn from this, and what will I do differently next time?* Try it—you'll be amazed at how these simple alterations will help you become guilt free.

Think in Technicolor

The *worrier* says: "I'm not good enough."

The *warrior* says: "I am enough."

"I am whole and perfect,
exactly as I am."

"I love me."

One day when I was five or six years old, my older sister and I were arguing about something, as we often did when we were kids. My father, an alcoholic, couldn't take the noise any longer. He stormed up to our rooms and yelled, "I'm so sick of you two kids fighting! I've had enough, and I'm giving you up for adoption." While my dad threw two suitcases down in the doorways of our adjoining rooms and told us to pack our bags, my sister and I stood silent.

My mind was racing. I imagined being dropped off on the cement front steps of a stranger's house, and I began to panic. My mom was at work, and I thought that she'd never be able to find me. I began to cry, and my dad said, "If you don't pack anything, you can go with nothing."

I walked over to the shelf at the far end of my room, picked up a teddy bear, went back over to the suitcase, and put it in. I wasn't sure if my sister packed anything. I was too scared and crying too hard to notice. Then my dad said, "Okay. I won't give you away this time, but if you two don't stop fighting, I will! And don't tell your mother." With those words, he returned to the basement.

It was in that moment that my perfectionism began. During that experience, I developed the belief that unless you're perfect, the people who are supposed to love you won't do so; and if you're not perfect, you're worthless and will be thrown away.

That's definitely not what my father had intended to accomplish. All he wanted was to get my sister and me to stop fighting so that he could have some peace and quiet. I have two daughters of my own now, and I fully understand how constant bickering can bring you close to the edge. My dad didn't want to hurt us. He never physically abused us, and he had no idea of his words' impact. Yet what he said did affect me, and I spent years struggling to meet an impossible standard and hating myself for falling short.

If you're a perfectionist, you may not be able to recall a specific situation that gave birth to your beliefs. In fact, it may not have been a single occurrence, but rather a series of events that culminated in the stifling burden. Whatever the cause, it's certain that perfectionism breeds worry.

Think of it this way, if you—like many women—are consumed by achieving an impeccable appearance, you'll likely brood over aging, your weight, or your wardrobe. If you're determined to never err where work is concerned, you may find yourself worrying about making mistakes, being rejected, losing the sale, or being anything other than number one in your field.

I realize that striving for excellence does have its place, and at times, high standards can serve you well. Trying to do your very best in life and taking great care certainly has its rewards. However, if you worry that no matter how hard you try, it's never good enough—that *you* are never good enough—then your perfectionism is working against you. To let go of this, think in Technicolor instead of black or white. When you see things only as black or white, good or bad, any little mistake feels like a total failure.

This is a common trap for many people who are trying to lose weight. Have you ever been on a diet, eaten something that wasn't on your program, and then said to yourself: *Well, now I've blown it?* Then, after mentally beating yourself up, you may have gone on a binge, all the while professing that tomorrow you'd start again, and stick to it perfectly this time? I've been there, done that! And for most perfectionist dieters, it happens again and again.

As ironic as it is, perfectionism can actually set you up for failure. Robert Schuller, in his book *Be Happy You Are Loved,* wrote a great sentence that you can repeat to yourself when perfectionism is lurking: "It's better to do something imperfectly than to do nothing perfectly!" Making a mistake is a good sign that you're doing something right—it proves that at least you're doing something!

Thankfully, the world isn't just black and white. It's purple, green, blue, magenta, aqua, orange, pink, red, mauve, yellow, and a multitude of other colors in between. It's time to think in Technicolor and add those hues to your life, which means changing the way you talk to yourself. To do so, catch yourself thinking: *I didn't do everything right,* and change it to *I may not have done everything right, but I didn't do everything wrong either.* It's a wonderful way to regain some perspective and halt the downward spin of unrealistically high expectations. Pay attention to what you demand from yourself. If you decide that there are some areas in your life where flexible standards will work better for you, start thinking in Technicolor and set your life up for success.

As for my dad, he's an amazing man, and I love him very much. He stopped drinking more than 20 years ago and hasn't had a drop since. He's a good father and a terrific grandfather. If you saw him playing hide-and-seek around the house with my daughters, you'd most likely agree. My dad is just like all of us—a person who has made mistakes and grown in the process. I'm proud of him, and I'm glad he's my father.

Looking back, I appreciate all the experiences I had growing up with an alcoholic parent because they made me who I am today—and I like myself just the way I am. You, too, are already good enough just the way you are right now. No number on a scale, in a bank account, or written in icing on a birthday cake will alter the wonder that is you. You don't need to search or struggle to be worthy, because you already are. Begin to believe it by affirming: *I am enough. I am whole and perfect exactly as I am. I love me.*

Release Judgments

The *worrier* asks: "What are they doing wrong?"

The *warrior* asks: "Are there some missing facts
that may help me understand
their point of view?"

"What is this prompting me
to recognize about my
own choices?"

"What changes can I make to
improve my own situation?"

Have you ever taken part in an auction? It can be quite exciting, especially if you're really interested in what's for sale. Imagine that you're at such an event and have just discovered that the item up for grabs is a live sea turtle. Attendees are bidding on the chance to *destroy* its beautiful, massive shell. Would you be excited to participate? I wasn't.

It was our first night on a beautiful island in the South Pacific, and my husband and I had joined 11 other vacationing couples for dinner on the beach. Right before the meal, we were told that some fishermen had captured a few hawksbill turtles that day, and the live animals would be auctioned off after dinner. The highest bidders would each win a chance to engrave a message on a turtle's shell. As the others were laughing and planning what they'd write if they won, I was thinking how terrible the whole thing was, and that I didn't want any part of it.

Before the auction began, the owner of the island came over to talk to us. He explained that hawksbill turtles are an endangered species, yet poachers still catch and kill the creatures for their highly prized shells. In an attempt to save the turtles, the owner had started a conservation program, where he buys the captured animals from fishermen and releases them, after first engraving a few marks on their shells. The carving doesn't harm the turtles in any way but renders their shells worthless. Because they're no longer of any value, poachers don't waste their time trying to catch them, and the turtles are left in the sea to reproduce. The auctions help raise enough funds to continue the catch-and-release program. Hearing this explanation, I realized that I'd assumed the worst—and I was wrong.

Have you ever passed judgment before you had all the facts? It's easy, but why do we do it? In part, I think we're attempting to feel better about ourselves. That's what I was doing at the turtle auction. I was trying to justify being on holiday without my two young daughters. My mind was fixed on our farewell at their grandparents' house, where the girls had been crying and begging me not to go. I was worried about how they were doing, and I was feeling pretty lousy about my decision to leave them. Trying to ease my own conscience, I focused my critical radar on the other couples and thought, *I may have left my kids with their grandparents, but at least I'm not as bad as these turtle destroyers.*

If you've ever judged another harshly in an attempt to make yourself feel better (as I did), you may have already figured out that it doesn't work. In fact, there are a number of reasons why it makes us feel worse.

1. When we criticize others, we usually focus on flaws and weaknesses, rather than on strengths. Anytime we dwell on negatives, it erodes our peace of mind and contentment, building inner turmoil and resentment.

2. What someone else has or hasn't done doesn't alter your actions. For instance, even if those "turtle destroyers" had actually injured the turtles for no apparent reason, it wouldn't have changed the fact that I left my kids to take my vacation. But in addition to feeling upset about my own decisions, I would have felt upset about others' choices—a double whammy!

3. The more harshly you judge others, the more critical you'll become about yourself. This is because you're really comparing them with you. You're holding up their choices, actions, and beliefs alongside yours. Anytime you compare yourself with others, you run the risk of being the one who comes up short. To top it off, you're likely to be most critical of others in the areas where you're the weakest. So when you condemn someone in an attempt to feel better about your own perceived shortcomings, you're really shining a mental spotlight on the things you dislike most about yourself.

The good news is that you have the power to turn it all around in an instant by choosing to be *curious* instead of *critical*—in other words, seek to understand rather than condemn. That doesn't mean you need to discard your opinions and beliefs. Instead, you'll gather all the facts, as best you can, with an open mind. Attempting to figure things out by adopting an open-minded curiosity puts you in a better position to learn from life's experiences, situations, and circumstances. As a result, you'll enhance your peace of mind and contentment.

There's another powerful benefit in releasing your judgments: The less you condemn others, the less you'll declare yourself unfit. You'll develop the habit of looking at every situation through a lens of curiosity—including your own situation. Consequently, when you think that you've fallen short, you won't have the need to beat yourself up over it. Instead, with greater self-love and self-acceptance, you'll be able to make positive changes while maintaining your inner calm.

If you find yourself harshly judging another, regain peace by shifting your thinking from critical to curious. Objectively gather all the facts, seek to understand rather than to find fault, and remember the hawksbill turtles—particularly the one swimming somewhere in the Pacific Ocean *with my name engraved on it!*

Accentuate the Positive

The *worrier* asks: "What might go wrong?"

The *warrior* asks: "What might go right?"
                     "What is the blessing?"
                     "What do I have left?"

It was 4:30 in the morning, five days before Christmas, when my phone rang. It was my mom, telling me that my grandfather had suffered a cardiac arrest.

I got dressed as quickly as I could and dashed to the car to make the two-hour journey to the hospital. I was relieved that it wasn't snowing; and I knew that the crisp, clear morning would make the drive itself relatively easy. But those hours of sitting behind the wheel, wondering whether or not my grandfather would survive—that was the hard part. The last time I'd received a call like this, my grandmother was in the hospital with cancer. She'd taken a turn for the worse, and I was told that I should come right away. She'd died while I was still en route, and I wondered if I were going to have the same experience all over again. I was afraid that my grandfather might be gone before I had the chance to hug him one last time and say good-bye.

When I arrived at the hospital, I quickly made my way to the cardiac-care unit, unsure of what I'd find. What I saw surprised me. My grandfather—hooked up to intravenous lines and a number of monitors, wearing an oxygen mask, and obviously experiencing a great deal of discomfort—was still his usual strong-spirited self. In fact, when the nurse told him that they needed to take a picture of his chest, he jokingly replied, "I'm not so sure I should let you. You might try to sell it on eBay." The nurse said, "I could use the extra money." He replied, "Okay, then, but let me autograph it first; it will be more valuable."

That "picture of his chest" showed that of the three main arteries exiting his heart, two were completely blocked and the third was 90 percent closed off. He needed an angioplasty to open up that third artery, and we were told that he might not survive the operation. Before the procedure, he looked at my mom and said, "Don't worry. I'm not going anywhere."

As I sat in the waiting room during the operation, it struck me that even in the middle of a life-threatening situation, it's possible to accentuate the positive, just as my grandfather was doing. Rather than focusing on the chance of dying, he was directing his thoughts to the possibility of surviving. That optimism made it a little easier for his family to endure the frightening event, and I believe that it also contributed to his recovery. He was discharged from the hospital in time to attend our family's Christmas dinner.

Many things in life that are difficult to endure—whether it's something as simple as a two-hour drive to the hospital on a clear morning, as challenging as surviving a life-threatening procedure, or anything in between—can be made easier simply by accentuating the positive. But how do you do that when you're smack-dab in the middle of a frightening event? The trick is to focus on what might go right instead of what could go wrong. This is an important skill to master, because when you dwell on what might not work out, you compound your worries. However, when you direct your thoughts in the other direction, you calm yourself.

Does focusing on what might go right mean that you pretend that negatives don't exist? Not at all—you simply avoid being consumed by them. Instead, you emphasize what's good, knowing that this will give you the hope, inspiration, and determination to believe in the possibility of a favorable outcome, and in doing so, soothe your worried mind.

A second way to accentuate the positive is to ask yourself: *What's the blessing?* There was a gift for my family hidden in this medical emergency: The ordeal united us during a Christmas season when we hadn't planned to be together. While our reason for gathering so close at Christmas could have certainly been better, it was nice to be together all the same.

There was also a benefit for my grandfather, as he learned to make healthy changes in his lifestyle, which may end up helping him live a longer life. In fact, five months after the surgery, I asked him what gifts the experience had given him. He said that he'd lost the excess 20 pounds he'd been carrying for years, his angina had cleared up, and he hadn't felt so well in quite a long time. When you look for the blessings in worrisome situations, the gratitude you feel will go a long way toward calming your mind.

Sometimes, when you're in the middle of a stressful event, finding the fortunate aspects of it can be a little tricky, as it was for me the time that I spent three-and-a-half hours on my computer writing a weekly segment for the television show I appear on. I'd been struggling for days to figure out how to say what I wanted to, and I was happy that I'd finally completed the task. Somehow, before I printed it, I deleted *everything.* I tried getting it back, but I couldn't. I called a computer expert to retrieve the data, but he couldn't either. It was gone. All my work and ideas were gone in the blink of an eye, with the push of a button.

I needed some consoling, so I phoned my husband. To help calm me down, he said, "It's okay. You created it, so it's still in you somewhere." Then, to make me feel better, he added, "Maybe it happened for a reason. Maybe when you rewrite it, it will be even better." He was using my own lessons on me! Let me tell you, when something bad has just happened to you, the last thing you want to hear is that it happened for a reason. But after getting past the initial shock of having lost hours of work, I realized that he was on target, and I did end up re-creating a wonderful segment after all.

My husband was right to focus on the bright side of a bleak situation. Don't get me wrong—I'm not suggesting that you need to be smiling all the time. Life has its ups and downs, and during those down times, it's okay to feel frustrated. But let's face it, as tempting as it can be, if you dwell on the negatives too long, you'll only feel worse.

In addition to focusing on what might go right and looking for the blessing, there's a third way to shift your outlook from negative to positive: Focus on what you have left. I think that Robert Schuller put it best in his book *Be Happy You Are Loved,* when he wrote: "Look at what you have left, never look at what you have lost."

I still had years of work left on my computer and my backup system. My situation could have been a lot worse. A computer virus could have wiped out my entire hard drive, but it didn't. Sometimes, however, what you've lost may be much greater than mere words typed on a screen. Does focusing on what you have left mean that you should forget what's gone? Not at all. Part of what remains is the memories, which are yours to keep. By shifting your focus to what you do possess, you don't get so consumed by what you've lost that you miss out on all the new memories yet to be created.

So the next time you find yourself in the middle of a stressful situation, accentuate the positive. Ask yourself: *What might go right? What's the blessing? What do I have left?* See for yourself how these three questions can help you shift your outlook from negative to positive, delete bad feelings, and calm your worried mind.

End "What-If" Thinking

The *worrier* asks: "What if?"

The *warrior* says: "What is?"
"Will it matter a year from now?"
"I will handle it!"

What if I get a flat tire on my way to the meeting? What if I don't have time to return all these e-mails and phone calls? What if I embarrass myself at the party? What if? What if? What if? It's remarkable how quickly these two little words can take over your thinking. If you give them the power to do so, they can cause many sleepless nights, a stomach full of knots, and seemingly unending mental turmoil.

In a previous chapter, you were taught to break free from "What-if" thinking by shifting your question from "Is it *possible* that what I'm worried about will happen?" to "Is it *probable*?" That simple modification can help you reconnect with your inner peace. In this chapter, you're learning to alter your inner dialogue so that it's nurturing. Because negative "What-if" thinking falls under the category of abusive self-talk, it's worth exploring two additional questions and an affirmation that you can use to change how you talk to yourself, free yourself from this harmful pattern, and take back your personal power. So, before you lose one more wink of sleep, allow that uneasy feeling in the pit of your stomach to linger a moment longer, or waste any more time and energy on "What-if" thoughts, try implementing these three cures:

1. Ask yourself: *What is?* This new question helps you stop borrowing trouble from the future and rehashing the past by focusing on the present. For instance, suppose you're worried about getting a flat tire on the way to a meeting. Stop the "What-if" game by reminding yourself that it's not happening to you right now. At this moment, you're safe, and you can check the spare tire in your trunk.

It's important to reframe the question to "What is?" because your brain doesn't know when you're actually in danger or just imagining potential hazards. When you conjure up frightening scenarios, your mind sets off the fight-or-flight response to keep you safe. This reaction is fabulous if you actually have to protect yourself. However, if the only thing you need refuge from is your own thinking, repeatedly triggering your survival instincts can take a toll on your physical health. Do your mind and body a favor by consciously redirecting your thoughts to the present moment and acknowledging that you're not in physical danger.

2. Ask yourself: *Will it matter a year from now?* Even if you do get a flat tire and turn up late for the meeting, will it really matter in 12 months? Will it make that much of a difference if your e-mails sit in your in-box for another day while you take some time out to enjoy your life, or to make progress on a goal you've had on the back burner for a while? Will that one small spelling mistake have catastrophic results? If you accidentally said the wrong thing at the company Christmas party, are you still going to be suffering a year later? Probably not. In fact, most of the things we spend our energy worrying about aren't that serious.

To distance yourself from current obstacles and concerns, ask yourself: *Will this matter a year from now?* This question will restore your perspective and remind you that most of the events in life that seem so urgent, stressful, and frustrating at the time are often insignificant in the grand scheme of things.

3. Affirm: *I will handle it!* If you feel that what you're worried about *will* matter a year from now, then affirm: *I will handle it!* Think about everything you've achieved up to this point in your life. Haven't you already managed to work with the cards that life has dealt to you? Isn't it true that you'll also be able to take care of whatever the future brings? Using this affirmation will help you build belief in your ability to deal with whatever comes your way. And once you believe that you can handle anything, you'll find that there really isn't anything to worry about.

The next time those "What ifs" are wasting your time and energy, focus on the present by asking: *What is?* Restore your perspective by asking: *Will it matter a year from now?* And build belief in your ability to manage whatever may come your way by affirming: *I will handle it!* These three cures will turn a worried mind into peace of mind.

Keep Your Hopes Up

The *worrier* says: "It's hopeless."

The *warrior* says: "I'm hopeful."
                     "Anything is possible."
                     "I believe in possibilities."

How do you think you'd react if a life were in danger? Would you panic or be levelheaded? It's difficult to predict exactly how you'd respond unless you've already experienced a life-or-death situation. I found myself in just such a predicament when I was 13 years old. It was winter, and I'd been playing on the ice of Lake Simcoe with two friends when I became bored and wandered off by myself. In an attempt to have some fun, I created a little game: I made piles of slush with my boots and jumped on them to splatter the slush. One of the heaps I made was massive. I knew that it would make a huge splash, and with great enthusiasm, I leaped on it. That time, I felt my knees get wet. I thought, *Oh no! I've fallen on the ice and now my pants are wet.* Just as I had that thought, I felt my hair swoosh up as though I'd plunged feetfirst into a swimming pool. That's when I knew that I hadn't fallen *on* the ice—I'd fallen *through* it.

What surprises me to this day is how I reacted at the time. I wasn't afraid, and I didn't panic. Instead, I felt a calm come over me. In this state, my mind became very clear. I thought, *Get your hands out of your pockets, take off your mittens and boots, then kick your feet so that you stay near the surface.* It was a really strange sensation, being so rational while my life was in danger. On top of being calm, I didn't even feel as though I were drowning. I know now that because the water was close to freezing, my body was already shutting down to protect itself.

While I was under the ice, one of my friends noticed that I was missing. She turned to the boy who was with us and asked, "Where's Denise?" After a quick scan of the area, they saw the hole. My friend instinctively ran over, plunged her arm into the icy water, and fished around until she found my hair. She grabbed hold of it, pulled me back up, and here I am today, safe and sound.

One thing I learned from the experience is that hope rises to the top. Along with calm and clear thinking, it kept me near the hole in the ice, which made it possible for my friend to rescue me. On the other hand, had I lost hope, panic would have surely set it. Fearful thoughts would have taken over and clouded my judgment. If that had happened, no matter how hard my friend tried that afternoon, she wouldn't have been able to reach me.

It's quite common to feel this unearthly calm when in a life-or-death situation—it's one way that the body/mind dynamic clicks into play. But how can you apply this knowledge to your everyday life? Chances are pretty good, on an average day, that you won't go through the ice or find yourself struggling to survive. However, life is sometimes slippery—metaphorically speaking—and once in a while, you may fall into a hole. From the breakdown of a relationship to an unfavorable health diagnosis, you'll encounter situations throughout your lifetime when your response will have a significant impact on your life. At those times, remember that panic sinks and hope rises up. The former creates fear and worry, which exhaust you, dragging you down physically, mentally, and emotionally. Hope, on the other hand, creates calm and restores your thinking. It lifts you up and pulls you through.

Choosing this positive emotion makes a great deal of sense, yet many women make a conscious decision against it. Why? They think that if they don't get their hopes up, they won't come crashing down, and as a result, they can avoid feeling disappointment, sorrow, and pain. This is reinforced time and time again with the common advice: "Don't get your hopes up."

The question you need to ask yourself is: *Why not?* Isn't having high hopes a much more pleasant way to live? And isn't it painful to live *without* a bright picture of the future? Isn't settling for fear and worry unpleasant? When you choose to forego hope, do you really keep yourself from suffering? No. What you avoid is a lot of wonderful opportunities and a life filled with happiness, satisfaction, and peace of mind.

How do you end this faulty logic? How do you regain your hope—even during those times when you feel you're in over your head? By believing that anything is possible. Having faith in possibilities is a message that's been featured several times throughout this book because it's a significant concept worth repeating.

Trusting that something good can happen will keep your hopes alive. Never give up, because anything is possible. Take, for instance, the time that I was invited to speak at the same two-day conference as Mary Higgins Clark—the best-selling author of suspense novels. When I found out that she was also on the bill, I was ecstatic! My imagination ran wild, and I began daydreaming about the incredible conversations we could have. On the first morning of the event, after presenting my workshop, I rushed over to the auditorium for Mary's keynote speech, where nearly a thousand women had already packed themselves into the room. My plan was to listen to the speech, then talk to her during the book signing that was to follow her presentation. Unfortunately, every other woman in the auditorium had the same idea.

I didn't have time to wait in the long line, so I headed back to my workshop room to prepare for my afternoon session. I was disappointed, but I didn't give up hope. After all, anything is possible; it was a two-day conference, and I still had the next day. I fell asleep that night trying to figure out how I could squeeze in a conversation with Mary.

Only a few hours after I drifted off, the hotel fire alarm sounded. I jumped out of bed, put my suit jacket on over my pajamas, grabbed my purse and my workshop materials—as if I could really present in my bunny-print flannel pj's—and made my way into the hall, down the stairs, and out of the hotel.

Outside, I saw that the fire department had already arrived. I was looking around in amusement at how silly we all appeared with our crazy, messed-up hair and wacky array of nightclothes when I spotted Mary Higgins Clark, standing alone beside the fire truck. I knew immediately that this was my chance, so I walked over and introduced myself to her.

As we were talking, I thought, *This is so cool! I'm having a pajama party with Mary Higgins Clark!*

Thirty minutes later, a firefighter interrupted our conversation and said, "It's safe to go back into the building." At which point, the Queen of Suspense turned to me, and with a mischievous look on her face, replied, "Or is it?" I'm telling you, I will treasure that experience for the rest of my life!

What is it that *you* are hoping for? From having a conversation with someone you admire to surviving a life-or-death situation, or anything in between, never give up! Don't ever tell yourself: *It's hopeless* or *I'm hopeless*. Never give up on your dreams and never give up on yourself. Decide today that you'll keep hoping in spite of disappointments, persevering in spite of obstacles, and believing in possibilities until your dreams happen for you. As I discovered in the middle of the night outside a hotel, standing beside a fire truck, it's often at the strangest time—when you least expect it—that your wishes come true.

How about your dream of letting go of worry? You've come a long way! You've learned to challenge your assumptions, act to control the controllable, let go of the uncontrollable, and master your mind. Now it's time to move on to the final chapter and put it all together.

Introduction

*One worry at a time, one step
at a time, and like magic, you'll
calm your worried mind.*

It's often been said that changing the world must happen one person at a time. Similarly, you can transform worry into inner calm, one anxiety—one step—at a time. To help make this transition a smooth one for you, this section of the book includes Transformation Tracking Sheets. These have the CALM process organized in an easy-to-implement format, allowing you to quickly apply the strategies you've learned in any given situation.

The sheets are set up with the four steps of the CALM process (below) listed in order. Under each one, you're asked a series of questions, which are designed to help you:

1. Challenge your assumptions.

2. Focus on solutions and gain the confidence and courage to take action to control what you can control.

3. Let go of those worries that are beyond your control by offering the strategies you've acquired in an at-a-glance format.

4. Master your mind by redirecting your thoughts from abusive to nurturing self-talk, and in doing so, transform yourself from a worrier into a warrior.

When you feel the first twinge of worry, begin working your way through the Transformation Tracking Sheets from top to bottom. It's important to realize that sometimes you won't need to apply every single step. In fact, maybe challenging your assumptions will be all it takes for you to regain your inner calm. Perhaps creating an action plan and following through will help you nip anxiety in the bud. Other times, a combination of two or three techniques will do the trick. Simply read each step and apply the ones that are relevant to your situation.

It's extremely beneficial to answer the questions on paper rather than in your head. Working your worries out on the page is a habit that will serve you well. It's much easier to identify and handle your thoughts and feelings when you write them down.

At the beginning, you may need to use the Transformation Tracking Sheets every day. You might find that you only experience inner calm for a brief amount of time, and then poof—another fear hits. That's okay. Take the time to restore your calm again. The more often you use this tool to regain your inner peace, the longer the calm feelings will last and the more the time between worries will grow. Eventually, you'll notice that the anxiety that once consumed you only shows up now and again. When it does, you'll be able to use the tracking sheets to quickly restore your inner peace.

You're going to be pleasantly surprised by how simple these Transformation Tracking Sheets are to use and how effective they are in calming your mind. I still use them myself when a worry pops up, and I'm always amazed by how fast they help me regain my inner peace. Take them as your personal template for worry-free living and you'll find that one worry at a time, one step at a time, you'll calm your worried mind.

Transformation
Tracking Sheets

*To restore calm: Challenge your assumptions,
act to control the controllable, let go of the
uncontrollable, and master your mind.*

Challenge Your Assumptions

- *What assumption(s) are you making?*

- *Whom can you talk to for a second opinion?*
  Remember to seek information from
  someone who will provide you with
  realistic, honest, and optimistic feedback.

- *Is it probable that what you're worried about
  will happen?* If so, move to the second step
  in the CALM process.

- *STOP! Are you starving (hungry), tired,
  ovulating (hormonal), or perturbed (upset)?*
  If so, realize that this may be the reason
  you're thinking and feeling the way
  you do, and then follow the suggestions
  previously provided.

- *What else could it be?* Your best line of defense for letting go of worry is to deal strictly with facts. Between now and the time it takes to get that data, make positive assumptions about the situation to regain your peace of mind.

- *Is it worry or intuition?* Remember that worry begins as a thought, and intuition begins as a feeling. Follow your intuition instead of your fears.

- *What are you afraid of losing?* If you're having difficulty challenging your assumptions, make sure you're dealing with the real issue by identifying what it is you're afraid of losing.

Act to Control the Controllable

- *Is this worry prompting you to take action?* If so, create a written action plan.

- *Is this action worth taking*? If so, affirm that you can do it, and then take action.

- *Is the fear of looking foolish stopping you from taking action?* Remember, the times in your life that you'll regret the most won't be when you looked foolish, but when you didn't take action at all.

- *Is the fear of making a mistake stopping you from taking action?* To overcome this anxiety, aim for success, not perfection.

- *Is doubt in possibilities stopping you from taking action?* Rather than focusing on what you can't do, concentrate on what you *can* accomplish. Believe in yourself and in the possibility that you can do what you set your mind to. Combine that belief with action, and never give up.

- *Are there actions you can take to influence the uncontrollable itself, the outcome, and/or the impact it has on your life?* If so, then take action.

- *Are you taking this action because it's right for you, or are you trying to please others?* If the fear of displeasing others or receiving criticism is stopping you from doing what you know is right for you, remember to consider the source, care about what you think of yourself, and look at the bigger picture.

- *Is this action in alignment with your definition of integrity?* If you've compromised your integrity, take actions to make amends if you can. If you're unable to do so, determine what you can learn from the experience and what you'll do differently if faced with the same situation in the future.

- *How will you feel tomorrow, next week, next month, or next year if you don't follow through?* Remember, the agony of regret outweighs the pain of following through.

Let Go of the Uncontrollable

What technique(s) will best help you let go? Use the following strategies:

- Act *as if.*
- Affirm the positive.
- Aromatherapy.
- Ask for help.
- Be adventurous.
- Be thankful.
- Be yourself.
- Breathe.
- "Busy" the worry out.
- Consume foods rich in vitamin B.
- Create a work of art.
- Declutter.
- Do what you're afraid of.
- Drink water.
- Eliminate worry-inducing words from your vocabulary.
- Exercise.
- Extend kindness to another.
- Find and utilize your unique ability.
- Focus on what matters.
- Focus on your accomplishments.
- Get a massage.
- Give a hug.
- Have faith in happy endings.
- Humor your worry.
- Immerse yourself in nature.
- Ink it.
- Listen to music.
- Make peace with your past.
- Meditate.
- Nurture yourself.
- Pay attention to your senses.
- Praise yourself.
- Pray.
- Read.
- Record your worry.
- Reduce caffeine.
- Relax your jaw.

- Rock.
- Say no.
- Schedule "worry time."
- Set a date to do something you love.
- Sleep well.
- Slow down.
- Spend time with a pet.
- Spend time with positive people.
- Step into the light.
- Talk to a friend.
- Trust yourself.
- Turn off the news.
- Visualize success.
- Volunteer.
- Walk.

Master Your Mind

- *Have you accepted responsibility for your state of mind?* Worry is a choice, so choose to release it, and make it your intention to live with peace of mind.

- *What are your limiting beliefs?* Identify the ones that you have about yourself by completing the following statements:

  "I'd be lovable if I . . ."
  "I'd be complete if I . . ."
  "I'd be deserving if I . . ."
  "I'd be wanted if I . . ."
  "I'd be adequate if I . . ."
  "I'd be okay if I . . ."

Next, write the word *opinion* beside every statement. The fact is that you already *are* lovable, complete, deserving, wanted, adequate, and okay . . . just the way you are.

- *What negative labels do you use to describe yourself?* Complete the statement: "I am . . ." For every negative label you have for yourself, write three positive statements.

- *Are you exaggerating or blowing this situation out of proportion with all-or-nothing thinking?* Write down what you're worried about, and then replace all-or-nothing words and phrases with more accurate truths.

- *Are you feeling sorry for yourself?* If something "unfair" has happened to you, try rewriting the scenario, and trust that every experience ultimately ends up serving you in a positive way.

- *Are you feeling guilty?* If so, release the guilt by asking yourself the following questions:

1. "Is the statement I'm hearing or the belief I'm holding 100 percent accurate?"

2. "Am I doing the best I can?"

3. "Is what I'm doing appropriate in this situation?"

4. "What actions can I take to make this situation more favorable?"

5. "What did I learn from this, and what will I do differently next time?"

- *Are your perfectionistic standards working against you?* If so, affirm to yourself:

  I am enough.
  I am whole and perfect exactly as I am.
  I love me.

- *Are you critically judging others?*
  If so, ask yourself:

  1. "Are there missing facts that may help me understand their point of view?"

  2. "What is this prompting me to recognize about my own choices?"

  3. "What changes can I make to improve my own situation?"

- *Are you focusing on what might go wrong instead of accentuating the positive?* If so, ask yourself:

    1. "What might go right?"
    2. "What is the blessing?"
    3. "What do I have left?"

- *Are you engaging in "What-if" thinking?* If so, ask yourself:

    1. "What is?"
    2. "Will it matter a year from now?"

    And affirm: *I will handle it.*

- *Are you feeling hopeless?* If so, affirm to yourself:

    I am hopeful.
    Anything is possible.
    I believe in possibilities.

Afterword

There you have it—the CALM process no longer simply refers to the words on the pages of a book; it's now a part of your thinking. You've acquired the skills to stop worrying, eliminate self-limiting beliefs, and develop greater inner peace. You've discovered strategies to *immediately* reduce anxiety and put an end to "What-if" thinking. You've found out how to transform fear into action and have learned how to finally stop dwelling on what others think of you. You know how to let go of perfectionism, regain excitement for life, and restore your peace of mind.

What does this mean? You now possess the key that enables you to quickly reconnect with the inner peace you desire and deserve anytime you choose. You're able to challenge your assumptions, act to control the controllable, let go of the uncontrollable, and master your mind so that you can stop worry the moment it starts. You can truly move forward in your life . . . relaxed, confident, and joy-filled.

I encourage you to continue to maintain your newfound calm. Use the strategies often, referring to them again and again until they're second nature. Share them with those in your life who also struggle with worry—your mate, children, siblings, parents, close friends, and casual acquaintances— so that they, too, can experience the inner peace you've come to know.

Finally, I encourage you to leap into your life and celebrate what you've already accomplished. Experience deep happiness and contentment for who you are today while anticipating the unlimited potential and abundance your future holds. This is a new path for you—one of worry-free living. Enjoy your life, fellow warrior—and enjoy the calm.

Acknowledgments

First and foremost, I thank my husband, Terry. I'm deeply grateful for your never-ending support, patience, encouragement, confidence, and most of all, for your love. You're a remarkable man, and I love and respect you with all my heart.

To my kindhearted and beautiful daughters, Lindsay and Brianna—you fill my life with love, joy, wisdom, inspiration, laughter, and magic. I thank you for all of it! Always remember how special you are and how much you're loved.

For my family, you have each contributed to the lessons and experiences that have shaped me into who I am today, and I'm grateful for each and every one of you. In alphabetical order, I extend my profound gratitude to Jim and Joan Allcock, Courtney Forbes, Murray and Betty Forbes, Murray and Laura Forbes, Bob and Jo-Anne Kite, Marion Kite, Deanna and Ted Thomas, Erin Thomas, and Nicholas Thomas. I also thank the Forbes, Geris, Marek, and Neabel families. I love you all!

My heartfelt thanks to my friends: Melissa Annan—you're an amazing woman; how lucky I am to call you my friend. Dan Carter and Paula Beebe—you're fantastic producers and even better friends; I'm blessed to have you in my life. Burt Henderson—you've been my personal trainer for nearly a decade, and over the years your integrity, friendship, and emotional support have made a significant difference in how I view myself and the world. Thank you. To Doug and Lisa McBride: Doug—I value our friendship and want you to know just how much you and your two incredible daughters mean to me. Lisa—even though your time on this earth was short, you impacted my life in a profound and beautiful way. Thank you. Deanna Thomas—I'm thanking you again because you're so much more than my sister; you're my beautiful, incredible friend!

I extend my deep appreciation to those individuals who have mentored me at different stages of my career: Kathleen O'Brien, Kai Rambow, Michael Smythe, Jason Stoll, and Christie Ward.

To the people who helped me during the publishing journey: Crystal Andrus—you truly are *simply woman!* I admire your strength and passion; thank you for your friendship! Nicholas Boothman—I thank you for your guidance and support; it's appreciated more than you know.

A huge thank you to my outstanding editing team: Katherine Coy, Jill Kramer, Shannon Littrell, Chris Morris, Bill Steinburg, and Jessica Vermooten.

Finally, I extend a special and abundant gratitude to Reid Tracy at Hay House. Thank you for believing in me and making it possible for this book to get in the hands of the women who need to let go of worry and who deserve to experience inner calm.

About the Author

Denise Marek is known as *The Worry Management Expert!* An international speaker and television personality, she has helped thousands of women transform their feelings of worry into inner peace. In June 2001, Denise earned the coveted Toastmasters International Accredited Speaker Award for Professionalism and Outstanding Achievements in Public Speaking. She lives in Ontario, Canada, with her husband, Terry, and their two daughters. For more information, visit: **www.denisemarek.com**.

We hope you enjoyed this Hay House book.
If you'd like to receive a free catalog featuring
additional Hay House books and products,
or if you'd like information about the
Hay Foundation, please contact:

Hay House, Inc.
P.O. Box 5100
Carlsbad, CA 92018-5100

(760) 431-7695 or **(800) 654-5126**
(760) 431-6948 (fax) or **(800) 650-5115 (fax)**
www.hayhouse.com®
www.hayfoundation.org

Published and distributed
in Australia by:
Hay House Australia Pty. Ltd.
18/36 Ralph St. • Alexandria NSW 2015
Phone: 612-9669-4299 • *Fax:* 612-9669-4144
www.hayhouse.com.au

Published and distributed
in the United Kingdom by:
Hay House UK, Ltd.
292B Kensal Rd., London W10 5BE
Phone: 44-20-8962-1230 • *Fax:* 44-20-8962-1239
www.hayhouse.co.uk